Also by Jamie Davis Whitmer

Haunted Asylums, Prisons, and Sanatoriums (Llewellyn, 2013)

America's Most

HAUNTED HOTELS

About the Author

Jamie Davis Whitmer is a writer, traveler, and investigator of lost things. She lives in Atlanta and Savannah, Georgia.

To Write to the Author

If you wish to contact the author or would like more information about this book, please write to the author in care of Llewellyn Worldwide, and we will forward your request. Both the author and the publisher appreciate hearing from you and learning of your enjoyment of this book and how it has helped you. Llewellyn Worldwide cannot guarantee that every letter written to the author can be answered, but all will be forwarded. Please write to:

Jamie Davis Whitmer
℅ Llewellyn Worldwide
2143 Wooddale Drive
Woodbury, MN 55125-2989

Please enclose a self-addressed stamped envelope for reply,
or $1.00 to cover costs. If outside the USA, enclose
an international postal reply coupon.

Many of Llewellyn's authors have websites with additional information and resources. For more information, please visit www.llewellyn.com.

JAMIE DAVIS WHITMER
with ROBERT WHITMER

America's Most

HAUNTED
HOTELS

Checking In *with Uninvited Guests*

Llewellyn Publications
Woodbury, Minnesota

FIRST EDITION
First Printing, 2016

Book design by Bob Gaul
Cover design by Lisa Novak
Cover images: iStockphoto.com/9453035©ilia-art
            Hotel by Jamie Davis Whitmer
Editing by Aaron Lawrence
Interior photos by Jamie Davis Whitmer, except on page 47 supplied by Chris Wilmoth, page 60 supplied by Steven Reed, and pages 105–106 (top only) supplied by Bill Ott

Llewellyn Publications is a registered trademark of Llewellyn Worldwide Ltd.

Library of Congress Cataloging-in-Publication Data
Names: Whitmer, Jamie Davis, author.
Title: America's most haunted hotels : checking in with uninvited guests / by
    Jamie Davis Whitmer.
Description: First Edition. | Woodbury, Minnesota : Llewellyn Worldwide,
    2016. | Includes bibliographical references.
Identifiers: LCCN 2016024296 (print) | LCCN 2016024504 (ebook) | ISBN
    9780738748009 | ISBN 9780738750101 ()
Subjects: LCSH: Haunted hotels—United States. | Ghosts—United States.
Classification: LCC BF1474.5 .W49 2016 (print) | LCC BF1474.5 (ebook) | DDC
    133.1/22—dc23
LC record available at https://lccn.loc.gov/2016024296

Llewellyn Publications
A Division of Llewellyn Worldwide Ltd.
2143 Wooddale Drive
Woodbury, MN 55125-2989
www.llewellyn.com

Printed in the United States of America

Contents

To my husband, who changed my way of life.

Introduction

By Jamie

I began officially looking for ghosts in 2008. In 2012 I wrote *Haunted Asylums, Prisons, and Sanatoriums* with my coauthor Samuel Queen, and it was published the fall of 2013. For that project, we traveled to and investigated ten locations with extremely haunted histories. If you enjoyed my first book, I think you will like this book, although it is certainly very different from my first project. There is an innate creepiness that goes along with abandoned hospitals and prisons that is not as blatantly obvious for haunted hotels. I also ask the reader to please bear in mind that there is a cost-of-the-project factor involved with investigating abandoned asylums versus investigating operating hotels. Remember that in order to actually *do* a paranormal investigation, you have to pay to shut the building down so you can control the investigation. Sam and I were able to do that in many of the locations we investigated for our first book because the cost was not so prohibitive. Many of the locations featured in *Haunted Asylums, Prisons, and Sanatoriums* cost less than $750 for the two of us to have full access to the building for twenty-four hours. It was not a cheap project, but it was something that was important to me. So when I was able to, I paid out of pocket and shut the show down for other players so I could get in there and investigate the building.

With hotels, you are talking about shutting down a viable business and buying out the occupancy for a day. To shut down even the smallest featured location in this book would have cost a minimum of $8,000 per night, and that unfortunately is beyond what my husband Bob and I can personally fund. In saying that, I would imagine that price point is beyond the capabilities of other people as well. So, we traveled and wrote and investigated to the extent possible under the limitations that are going to exist for the average guest. I think that has value because you can read this book from a real person's perspective. This is a nonfiction work written from a working-class person's perspective. This is not a fantasy investigation report of what only someone with an unlimited travel budget could make happen. My best tip for bookings if you are trying to get into one of these places and wind up alone in the building is to look at the first week of January, just after the New Year's holiday celebrations. This strategy worked for us at the Myrtles Plantation and at the Jerome Grand Hotel.

Hotels are strange places. One of the creepiest things about any hotel, regardless of its history, is the hallways. There is something unsettling about a long, dimly lit hallway of a hotel. You are surrounded by what appears to be an unending line of closed doors. You have no idea what is behind any of them, or who—or what—could be watching you as you walk a seemingly empty hall. People are passing through hotels constantly, and sometimes all of this traffic can leave emotions behind as residual imprints.

Interestingly enough, many of the locations we covered have rich histories of being used as hospitals, although I have to tell you that I did not specifically set out to find them when our journey started. There are stories of mysterious deaths, murders, and suicides connected with the hotels featured in this book. The RMS Queen Mary was a war ship that collided with the HMS Curacoa in 1942, resulting in 338 deaths. Many believe that this accident has contributed heavily to the paranormal reports on the ship. The Kehoe House was a former funeral home. Every hotel that is featured has been heavily reported as "haunted," either by the locals or the national media, and many times a combination thereof. All of the locations I scouted and chose to feature have signed photo releases, all are open-minded about their respective paranormal legends (many are more than open-minded and outright encourage the exploration of the subject), and most are smaller venues. Some are even small family businesses.

My opinion after researching and traveling for two books is that the former hospitals seem to be the most actively haunted places. My theory for this: when you go into a hospital, you go in at least with the expectation that you're going to be saved. People who are confined inside prisons and asylums know that they have already lost. It is almost as though the energy does not feel as desperate and that there is a resigned feeling.

It has been vastly claimed that the entire towns that contain some of the highlighted hotels are haunted (for instance, Savannah, Georgia; Jerome, Arizona; Gettysburg, Pennsylvania; and Bisbee, Arizona). Geology and history combine in many cases to support the legends of the hauntings discussed. My husband and I wanted to explore some of these famous locations and attempt to draw a line between fact and fiction. Folklore is a huge part of ghost stories, but we were able to find that the truth is sometimes stranger than fiction. For instance, the legend of Norman Baker and the history of the famous 1886 Crescent Hotel is one such truth that I find to be stranger than fiction.

For this project, I set out to obtain more firsthand witness interviews. We also tried out some new equipment. I bought a Mel Meter, a green laser grid light, and a SB7 Ghost Box.

As I have evolved in my own reading and studying, my objective for this project has grown much deeper than the objective of my first book. One of the works that I read before we started traveling was James Van Praagh's *Ghosts Among Us*. In this book, Van Praagh discusses spirits being either "in the light" or "earthbound." The spirits in the light are those whose souls are vibrating on a higher energy level. There are many experiences within this book that deeply resonated with me, and I wanted to make sure that we were doing the work on ourselves to keep our energy levels high and pure before we started poking around in the great unknown. The universal law that like attracts like is very real to us. So this time I did not go seeking an answer to a general call of "I'm here to talk to anyone who wants to talk to me." My purpose on this journey was to examine history and legends but also to seek contact only from those spirits who are "in the light." I avoided calling the darker earthbound souls to us. Also, because of my deeply moving and personal experiences from the first time I set foot in the Crescent Hotel and the town of Eureka Springs, I wanted to do some more research into the possibility of past lives. I will talk briefly about it later, but let it suffice for now that Bob and I believe we have known each other before. It is an interesting and comforting belief that there are key people in all of our lives—soul mates, if you will—whom we are always traveling with, over and over again through time. Like Van Praagh says, "There are no mistakes." I also believe that we have guides and that we are sometimes able to get in contact with them.

Travel and my experiences—these are my truths. These are the things that I have spent money on and never regretted it because they have enriched my life. Everything else seems like noise and other people trying to push their agendas on me. I like motion. I like the illusion of freedom. I would encourage you to seek and find your truth through your own personal experiences.

There is magic in travel. While there is no denying the importance of your destination, much of the magic is involved in the act of travel in and of itself. Whoever you are at home, there are certain roles and perceptions that everyone in your life has of you. For instance, if you are a teacher who is also a mother, that is how the community labels and defines you, and maybe it's even the identity you define for yourself. However, when you travel, something magical happens. You become in tune with your innate self and can hear who you are again. You are a man or a woman, a person with his or her own unique set of abilities, hopes, and dreams. No one knows you. You are able to just "be." Sylvia Plath said it best in "Two Campers in Cloud Country" when she wrote, "It is comfortable, for a change, to mean so little" (1971). I think she was describing the peace she finally felt when she realized that nothing really matters here. Am I being flippant? Maybe. But think about it. There is nothing else *but* being. Once I realized that, I felt peace for the first time in my adult life. Everything else we do to fill the time and make money is just something we either pick purposefully or wind up doing by chance until we die. We are all attempting to fill the great empty with meaning.

This book is as much about the joy of travel and leisure as it is about exploring haunted hotels.

I hope you will find this book inspiring and enjoyable and that you will drop me a line about some of your own haunted adventures. You are my fellow traveler, and you are on a journey to somewhere else.

By Robert "Bob"

When I first agreed to do this book with Jamie, I did so with a little uncertainty and more than a little discomfort, as I did not know what to expect. My religious upbringing forbade any belief or discussion of these things, and that conditioning predisposed me toward a cautious stance, which is not a bad thing. I believe there is some risk involved with ghost hunting, and I will admit that there is still considerable discomfort in the matter. I am not comfortable being around beings of conscious energy that I cannot see. I believe there are spirits out there that have never been human and not all are friendly. Even dipping a toe in these waters can be dangerous.

What I have come to believe, however, at least in the vast majority of cases, is that ghost hunters and paranormal researchers are dealing with human souls in varying states. I believe the human soul is energy that cannot be destroyed. Reading numerous accounts of near-death experiences and many other sources of information, I have come to believe that what happens after death may not be exactly as they taught in church.

I believe the human soul experiences life in the five-sense dimension. Life in physical rather than spiritual form is much more vivid and intense. The sensations involved with feeling a warm breeze, eating a delicious meal, or falling in love are something that I believe can only be experienced while in a physical form, which is why the will to live is so strong. Life is more intense, but it also limits us to much tighter fields of awareness. We are spiritually limited while in a physical form. When the person dies, he or she is no longer bound to the five-sense limitations and can move between dimensions, often going to a spiritual dimension that is in resonance with the vibrational energy of the person's soul. Some souls are kind and gentle, while some are much less so. Sometimes these dimensions cross over into ours, whether by choice or by circumstance.

Skeptics tend not to believe things they cannot experience with the five senses. If they cannot see, feel, touch, smell, or hear something, then it must not exist. But since the universe exists as electromagnetic energy in incredibly varied forms across an incomprehensibly huge spectrum, the tiny spectrum we can sense with our five senses is like looking at the universe through a drinking straw. To deny the existence of anything outside the view of that drinking straw is foolish.

I am open to the possibility that things exist that I cannot see, but despite the fact that I question the wisdom of chasing these things around dark hotels, I go into this endeavor with an open but cautious mind. It is not my goal to convince the reader in any way; it is more to give an honest assessment of what I experienced in the following chapters. I am neither a skeptic nor a zealot, but rather a fellow traveler with my amazing wife as we explore a paradigm quite foreign to my logical mind.

ONE

The Myrtles Plantation
St. Francisville, LA

New Orleans is the only place I have ever visited where I have actively felt evil or dark energy. This includes Las Vegas and a whole host of abandoned prisons, hospitals, and asylums. New Orleans wins hands down every single time. If you are shopping for antiques and art on Royal Street, you may not feel it. But New Orleans is the only city I have ever traveled to where the bus-tour salesman's biggest pitch was, "Be careful out there. This city is the murder capital of the world. People look the same out here, but they're not." A few short hours later, we met a walking zombie while exiting one of the galleries on Royal Street late in the afternoon. I noticed him a few shops back, but I mistakenly thought he was cursing and following some other tourist in front of us. It turned out that the zombie was stuck on us the whole entire time. He was having a heated debate with someone we could not see.

The exterior of the Myrtles Plantation.

We dipped down a side street beside the St. Louis Cathedral to hide from him, but he followed us again. He passed us, and when he got a few yards ahead, he turned around and his black, lifeless eyes locked eyes with me. His message? "You staring. You're next."

New Orleans is a strange place. We hid out for the night and ordered room service. I tried to relax, but the stranger's words were haunting me. I could not help but think about the words he told me and the way his black eyes locked with mine. Sometimes there are no such things as random coincidences. Part of being in tune with the universe is learning the difference between actual messages and signs and a meaningless exchange that takes place with someone else. I measure the signs and exchanges by how they make me feel. It was an intense moment, and I spent the night wondering if the message was meant as some type of warning. I was, after all, on the eve of hunting ghosts again. (Check out *Haunted Asylums, Prisons, and Sanatoriums* for details on my first run-in with a zombie.)

The next day would take us to St. Francisville and the famous Myrtles Plantation, where we would be the only guests for the night. We could not know it at the time, but things were about to get even weirder.

History

The Myrtles Plantation was built by David Bradford in 1794. The house has a timeline of events and owners that is quite extensive. For the sake of simplicity, ownership appears to go from Bradford to Woodruff in 1817, then to the Stirling family in 1834. Next, it goes to Winter through marriage in 1852, and after that, there are a series of different owners.

Frances Kermeen owned the home from 1980 to 1990, and she authored *Ghostly Encounters* in 2002, which contains a chapter about the Myrtles. She then authored *The Myrtles Plantation* in 2005. One of the things she wrote about was how the Tunica Indians considered the land to be a sacred place, and she calls it a spiritual vortex.

The Myrtles Plantation outlines some of the paranormal experiences that Kermeen had while living in the plantation as well as events that happened to other friends, family members, and guests. The reports range from the mundane to the incredibly hard to believe, and they include seeing the apparition of a former servant carrying a candle throughout the house at night and tucking people in; waking up to heavy footsteps that sound like heavy boots walking; a bed that levitates; portraits that shed real tears; and a combination of ghost sex and ghost rape.

Kermeen wrote that the man she purchased the home from only owned the property for three years before she bought it. He sold it so he could leave and join a monastery. When she moved in, she noticed little odd details about the home, such as bags of salt underneath all of the windows and upside down keyholes for the doors. She was told by a staff member that both things were used to ward off evil spirits. She was also informed that the graveyard had been paved over to build a parking lot. We were told by staff on our tour that they do not know where the historic grave-yard is.

One of the most fascinating themes that Kermeen writes about is how she felt that fate or destiny had a hand in leading her to own the home, and she talks about her intense possible past-life connection with Sarah Mathilda. She claimed that she had a powerful feeling of déjà vu when she first saw the back staircase, and she even had some weird dreams while staying at the home prior to her official purchase date. She also claimed that a voodoo curse was placed on her in Haiti just before she happened upon the house for the first time.

John and Teeta Moss are the current owners, and they purchased the home around Christmas in 1992. There is a short four-minute interview of the two of them on YouTube where they address some of the haunted history of the home. Mrs. Moss has inexplicably experienced her name being called, seemingly in her husband's voice (when it was not her husband calling her). Mr. Moss said that he does believe in guardian angels.

Visiting the Myrtles

The Myrtles looks and feels just like the stately and elegant image of the haunted Southern mansion that I always had in my mind when I would devour ghost stories as a child. It is beautifully (and I imagine lovingly, based on the appearance of the home) preserved using period decorations. Some of the original interior elements of the home that have been saved include a three-hundred-pound Baccarat crystal French chandelier; a stained-glass door, "hand-painted, etched, and patterned after the French cross to ward off evil"; Carrara marble; and frieze work molding ("History of the Myrtles Plantation").

The first thing we did was walk around the exterior of the home and the grounds with the Mel Meter to see if we could get any hits or notice any big changes in temperature. Right off the bat, Bob watched the Mel Meter jump to register a 6.8 when he held the meter against the door leading into our room, the General Bradford Suite, which was off the porch. We completed our walk around the property and my phone died when we got to the left side of the home. I was at 60 percent power and then it was suddenly completely dead when we passed the old caretaker's cottage. When we returned to the door off the porch again that would lead us to our room, we took another reading with the Mel Meter. Nothing happened. We thought that was a little strange. The inability to obtain the same results made us think that the first measurement could possibly be attributed to something paranormal. When we entered the room and plugged my phone back in, it came right back to life—this time with 61 percent power.

I noticed that the shutters of the home appeared to be painted in a shade of haint blue, and so was the elaborate ironwork on the front porch. I first learned this term on a tour in Savannah, Georgia. The haint-blue paint shade was created by mixing indigo, lime, and buttermilk, and it was used on ceilings, around windows and doors, and even behind or under the furniture. In Gullah culture, spirits are not able to cross water, so the paint was used as protection against evil spirits. We noticed that many homes in the Garden District of New Orleans were covered in shades of haint blue as well. It is fascinating to see this tradition still in effect in modern times.

We got extremely lucky when booking our stay in early January, and we wound up having the entire house to ourselves. It was mild for January, and I spent some time relaxing in one of the rocking chairs on the 125-foot-long veranda. This is a prime spot to listen to the sounds of the centuries-old oak trees and ponder over all the events and energy that they have seen and soaked up over the course of the home's 221 or so years.

The porch of the Myrtles.

We took advantage of the daytime historic tour that is offered complimentary to all guests with their overnight bookings. We were told some of the popular ghost stories on this tour because our guide knew we were there to write this book, but normally they reserve the ghost stories for their mystery tours, which are held on weekend nights.

I love a good story as much as anyone, and maybe even more so, and of course folklore is a huge part of this subject matter. However, I also enjoy and appreciate finding real pieces of history to savor and use to help understand current events and reported happenings. There are a lot of rumors and very old stories that surround the hauntings at the Myrtles.

On March 29, 2015, I sent an e-mail to the house and asked for their comment about the truth versus legend controversy surrounding the famous Chloe and the Myrtles. This was owner Teeta Moss's response:

"There is no historical evidence that 'Chloe' was the name of the house servant who was also a nanny to the children because none of the slaves were named in the historical records. The name was given to her as the folklore and legends were passed down through the generations. It is a possibility that is the name she was called but there is no proof."

I thought that was a great e-mail. After all, the owners cannot control rumors or what other people write about their location on the Internet!

I specifically asked our guide if he could comment on all of the allegations that Kermeen made in her book, and his comment was that he had not heard any modern claims of the more disturbing haunted allegations that Kermeen claimed to experience during her period of ownership. So rest assured; it has been a long, long time since anyone has claimed to take a ride on a levitating bed.

As mentioned, probably the most famous spirit legend associated with the home concerns "Chloe." We were quick to get the scoop from our guide.

Sarah, the "Poisoned" Children, and "Chloe"

One of the most popular stories about the house that has been passed down is that Sarah Mathilda Woodruff and her two children were poisoned by one of their slaves in the early 1800s. This rumor seems to be the origination of the "Chloe" character. The popular story accuses Clark Woodruff of carrying on an affair with one of his house slaves. He allegedly caught her eavesdropping one day and ordered one of her ears to be chopped off. She started wearing a green turban to cover her injuries. The girl allegedly took her revenge by mixing deadly oleander into a birthday cake. Depending on the storyteller, the intent was either to poison the wife and children just a little bit to make them sick so she could swoop in as a nurse and save the day, regaining favor within the household, or the intent was premeditated murder to exact revenge. Whatever the intent, the story goes that the family died by the hands of Chloe. Afterward, the other slaves captured Chloe and hung her from a tree in the yard until she was dead.

Over the years, countless witnesses have claimed to see the apparition of Chloe and the children. People report that they have been awakened by Chloe or that they have seen her walking around the home wearing a green turban. The children have been seen playing in the yard, and there are photographs of them on the roof as well as photographs of them peering out of a window in the house (these are on the Myrtles's website).

There is even compelling photographic evidence of the ghostly apparition of Chloe that was purportedly authenticated by both the National Geographic Explorer filming crew and a patent researcher by the name of Norman Benoit. The gift shop at the Myrtles sells the photo as a postcard, and it is linked to their website with the story. It does appear to me that a ghostly image of a slave girl was captured in the photograph! She appears to be traveling from the main house to the kitchen.

But who *is* the mysterious female that everyone calls Chloe? You read the above e-mail excerpt from the current owner that there is no historical evidence to support the existence of a real-life Chloe. Troy Taylor, well-respected author, investigator, and president of the American Ghost Society, has also claimed to have conducted extensive research to uncover the real Chloe.

Taylor's book *The Haunting of America* contains an entire chapter that compares the facts that he has found to many rumors circulated about the home, and many of the stories simply do not jive as far as being supported by actual documents. Taylor reported that Sarah Mathilda died from yellow fever on July 21, 1823. Her son James passed on July 15, 1824, and Cornelia Gale succumbed in September 1824. Taylor goes even further and wrote that the property records on file with St. Francisville list the names of the slaves owned by the family and Chloe (or Cleo, for that matter) is not one of them. In her 2005 book, Kermeen backtracked on this issue and wrote on page 162 that she conducted her own research into courthouse records and found that Sarah and her two children actually all died of yellow fever. Note that this is vastly different from what she first wrote in her 2002 book, which also perpetuates many of the popular tall tales. In her 2002 version of the story, she sticks with the story that Chloe unwittingly poisoned them. However, I found that both Kermeen and Taylor agree in their latest writings that the family died from yellow fever, not from any poisonings.

Even though the stories do not appear to be based on historical facts, there have still been countless sightings and witness reports of Chloe and the children. There is no denying that people have been and are continuing to experience something that they cannot easily explain. It is human nature to put a name and a story together to help explain what it is that you are experiencing. What's more, Taylor also suggests that the story could have originated from the 1950s when family stories began to circulate about an old woman spirit who was seen around the house. That woman was said to wear a green bonnet.

William Winter

There are many writings on the Myrtles, but in the interest of full disclosure to you regarding my own independent research, I was unfortunately unable to stay in St. Francisville indefinitely so I could duplicate Taylor's efforts and perform my own research. As a caveat, that goes for all of the locations I visited. Without being able to do that, it is impossible for me to seriously enter an opinion on the record as to what is "truth" and what is "legend." I caution you against truth in the conclusion to this book. Just because there is no document that exists from 1800 does not mean that something did not occur. As Bob says, "Absence of evidence is not evidence of absence."

I can at least honestly disclose my limitations to you, though, and let you determine for yourself whether you wish to engage in your own manner of private research.

There were many natural deaths that occurred inside the home, but there was only one murder in the main house that I could verify, and that was the murder of William Winter.

The legend claims that William Winter was shot and then died of his injuries while walking up the stairs of the home. Upon reaching the seventeenth step, he collapsed in Sarah Mathilda's arms and died. Stories were written and published that alleged that his phantom footsteps could be heard laboring up the staircase, only to disappear once he reached the seventeenth step. To this day, common reports are made that guests have heard heavy footsteps walking up and down the main staircase. Our guide opined that the entire stair area of the home has been labeled a portal, or a time warp, and that many believe spirits travel through this common area. At the bottom of the main stairs, there is a heavy antique mirror that hangs on the wall. Some people believe that the mirror trapped the spirits of the people who died at the Myrtles. If you take a picture, you just might find that your image contains their handprints, seemingly trapped behind the glass!

The possible truth behind the legend of William Winter comes from a historic newspaper article. According to a January issue of the *Point Coupee Democrat*, a stranger called on William Winter, claiming he had business with him. Winter stepped out onto his front porch, was shot by the stranger, and died on the porch on January 26, 1871, not on the stairs (Taylor and Wiseheart, 2015). Of course, it is completely feasible that people have heard phantom footsteps on the stairs. Whether or not they can be attributed to William Winter's spirit is anyone's guess. If it is him, I prefer to think of it as residual energy that is playing in a time loop.

I don't want to believe in a world where a husband is trapped in a never-ending circle of spirit hell where he consciously reenacts his death and then struggles to make one last attempt to see his wife before succumbing to gunshot wounds. If anything, surely this phenomenon is a residual imprint that is caused by the trauma. I did not come across any stories of anyone interacting with an intelligent spirit that they thought was William Winter. Sarah, William's widow, went into a deep state of mourning after her husband's death. She wore black the rest of her days, ate little, and essentially grieved herself to an early death at the age of forty-four.

Caretaker Murder

There was a murder of the caretaker on the property, but not in the main house. He said the caretaker was Eddie Haralson, the brother of Fannie Williams, and he was living in the small cottage behind the main house when he was killed in a robbery that occurred in 1927 (2015).

Our guide wrapped up our tour and we watched the other customers slowly dwindle away from the crowd and return to their cars, leaving us alone for the night at the Myrtles.

Evening Sets In at the Myrtles

By 4:50 p.m. on a Sunday night, it was already getting dark. The Carriage House Restaurant was closed (they offer a brunch on Sundays), and the staff began making their way off the property. The cold was moving in now and it was raining. We heard a howling noise as the wind began to rally and gear up for the night, and a shutter outside our room slammed shut. The scene was set.

We had the run of the home as far as the guest bedrooms that night, and I just knew that we were going to be in for an interesting night based on how creepy the Fannie Williams Room—the "doll room"—looked. We had been told a frightening story about that doll; namely, she situates herself around that room sometimes when you are not paying attention to her.

The upstairs hallway outside of the guest rooms.

The Fannie Williams room.

Despite our attempts at active ghost hunting within the home that night, nothing strange happened to us while we were awake and actively looking for something to happen. We began in the dark in the doll room and lined our equipment up across the room from where we were sitting. I was using a digital voice recorder, three twist-top flashlights, a K-II meter, and our Mel Meter. I usually start the session with a short introduction of who we are, why we are there, and then I state that we would like to talk with anyone whose intent matches ours. What I mean by that is someone with pure or good intent. We do not provoke, and we do not want to talk with any mean-spirited entities. We believe that like attracts like, and we believe that if you keep your intentions in the light, you will attract like-minded spirits.

After I make the introduction, I like to get into asking about any specific people or stories that we have heard about to see if we can make contact with anyone. I led by asking for Chloe. I began by saying, "We heard stories this afternoon about Chloe. Is Chloe here? Chloe, if you are here, can you use one of those flashlights to let us know? Just twist the top end, and it should light up and we will know you are here. Or, if you are having trouble with the flashlight, see if you can move close to that gray box over there in the corner. We call that a K-II meter and it should light up if you get close to it. It is thought to be able to measure your energy! The black box that you see is a recorder. If you step close to it and say your name when I stop talking, I will play it back and see if I can hear you. Okay, try it." (Stay silent for at least thirty to sixty seconds to give enough time to answer.)

I like to do electronic voice phenomenon (EVP) sessions in short bursts, namely because I love the instant gratification of it but also because it is just too hard for me to pick up anything out of the background from hours of listening to audio. Some people have a real talent for picking up voices out of the white noise, but it can honestly all sound so unclear to me. Also, remember that you can only do meaningful EVP sessions in a building where you know you are the only people there. Otherwise, you could just be picking up your neighbor's conversation in the hotel room next to you.

After trying to reach Chloe, I asked for William, and then Sarah, and then the two children, James and Cornelia. I then opened the session to communicating with any travelers—anyone who might be passing through who can hear us and might want to talk to us. I sat and waited, talked, and asked for a sign for a few hours, but there was nothing going on that we could notice or feel that evening. Sometimes while having conversations with each other, we might get some activity like a flashlight lighting up or a K-II meter lighting up as though someone is joining in on the conversation. My belief is to conduct the sessions or conversations as though you are having a first conversation with a person at a party or exchanging some witty banter with a coworker. Sometimes I will forget to watch my slang or jargon, and I think that can sometimes impede progress. A spirit from the 1800s who still thinks that they are in that time period does not know what I am talking about when I use modern slang. Bob will nudge me when I start to lapse into slang territory.

Bob opined that maybe we were dealing with highbrow plantation owner spirits, and they were looking down their noses at us. He said he thought maybe we were dealing with some personality differences between the inhabitants of the Myrtles and the inhabitants of the asylums and prisons I had previously visited, where the spirits were practically jumping up and down and turning flashlights on in response to my questions during the first few minutes of my sessions.

There might just be something to that. This time we were in someone's house, and they did not seem to be anywhere near as anxious to make contact with us.

We slept in the General Bradford Suite, complete with antique furnishings, lace, and the distinct smell of history. I think there is a pure wood smell that comes from old houses, and I absolutely love it. With no other living souls in sight and no snacks to speak of, we bedded down for the night, and in my opinion, mostly passed the night uneventfully. Bob would later report otherwise.

I slept until about 5:00 a.m. when I woke up to the sounds of someone rustling around our room near the bed—specifically, it sounded like skirts rustling, and the sound was close to my face—followed by heavy boot steps approaching the room to the door off the porch. The boots were slow, determined, and strong. *Clomp, clomp, clomp.*

I then heard what sounded like four wild cats losing their minds, howling as though they were facing death itself out there, while at the same time maintaining a constant run away from whatever was on the porch.

But there was nobody outside and no cars in the parking lot. By this time I was realizing just how cold the bedroom was. It was down to around fifty-five degrees, but the heat was still running. The front parlor of our suite had dropped down to the mid-sixties.

The heat was working splendidly when we arrived and when we went to bed. I had left the temperature at seventy-two degrees when I went to sleep and woke a few hours later to a room that had dropped to fifty-five degrees. Bob would later tell me that he watched the temperature drop on the Mel Meter in real time.

I know that it was winter and it's not uncommon to have heating problems such as those we experienced. Old wooden houses get cold and old heaters break. I also know that people hear weird stuff when they think they are awake but are really still dreaming. But why in all my years can I not recall a dream where I have had auditory hallucinations? Do I only hallucinate while sleeping in haunted mansions, or was something really going on? I am inclined to believe that something real was going on. This was not a dream.

The General Bradford Suite.

Seeing that I was also awake, and freezing, Bob let me in on what happened to him earlier during the night while I had been sleeping peacefully right beside him.

Comments from Bob

The Myrtles Plantation experience was the most unnerving yet fascinating experience in recent memory. From the moment we arrived in our room, I felt a very uneasy and uncomfortable sensation. The sensation that something was very wrong combined with an unexplained cold clamminess to the air made it feel very haunted. It felt like it was surrounding me. Based on this feeling, I can understand where the theory of ectoplasm fits into paranormal discussions. It feels like this gooey substance is moments away from forming and coating me. It was a sensation that would become familiar and instantly recognizable in our travels.

The Mel Meter was our most vital tool in the Myrtles because it showed frequent readings that were not consistent; thus they could not be explained away as picking up something from the atmosphere like electrical currents from a cable in a wall. Despite our attempts to get the spirits to light up the flashlights, these spirits didn't want to play that game. No, these spirits were not interested in playing games—at least not our games. They had some games of their own in mind for us.

Whatever was at the Myrtles was decidedly different. They were in charge, not us. The Mel Meter picked up several very strong readings one moment but were gone the next. We also picked up numerous strong but intermittent signals at the bottom of the stairway. The stairway was said to be a portal area, so maybe that is what we were picking up. While the premises were definitely eerie, we picked up no discernible activity other than the Mel Meter readings. Later that night, things would change.

While getting ready for bed, I accidentally spilled about a half cup of water on the nightstand next to the bed. This may have upset the territorial resident spirits because at about 1:00 a.m., I awoke with a very uneasy feeling, and I was freezing! I turned on the Mel Meter, which has a built in thermometer. I watched as the temperature dropped approximately one degree Fahrenheit every five or six seconds. It went from seventy to fifty-five degrees in about a minute. I had a strong sense that we were not alone.

The Mel Meter has a record feature that can be activated and later analyzed for spikes in the readings. I activated the record button before trying to get back to sleep. We awoke at about five a.m. to a loud bang, which I attributed to the wooden shutters opening violently and slamming against the house. Seconds later, a group of nearby cats started behaving unlike anything I had ever heard. They were howling and screeching and very unhappy about something! This accompanied the loud sounds of boot footfalls on the front porch—the same front porch where the murder took place. Something was out there and was obviously not happy, and we were feeling quite on edge.

We noticed that the Mel Meter, which had been recording on the nightstand about a foot from my head, and about six inches from where I spilled the water, had picked up a very strong reading sometime in the night. I also had a scratch on my forehead that had not been there the night before. I suspect my clumsiness upset the local residents and they wanted us gone.

We took some photos of the plantation grounds, thanked our very gracious hosts, and then departed mid-morning. It is a good thing we don't scare easily.

Jamie's Final Thoughts

We left with the opinion that someone or something had definitely been checking us out but was not interested in interacting with us. Maybe the footsteps were just residual. An entry from my journal on the morning of our departure from the Myrtles, which was written in the car on our way out of town, is as follows: "When I woke up this morning, I felt really sad. I sat on the chair in the front parlor and cleared my mind so I could concentrate on the feeling. All these places we've gone to, I've never really felt my own death, but it was very much on my mind this morning, and I was concerned about losing Bob. I felt the sudden urge to cling to him, as though acutely aware that one day, sooner than I wanted, he would leave me. He would die, and I would be left here, alone, essentially with nothing. I wonder if I was being an empath to one of the widows—Mary Catherine or Sarah? We're both feeling better as we get further and further away from the Myrtles."

If You Decide to Visit

Location & Contact Info

7747 U.S. Highway 61

St. Francisville, Louisiana 70775

Tel: 225-635-6277

E-mail: *chloe@myrtlesplantation.com*

Website: *http://www.myrtlesplantation.com/index.html*

Type of Tours & Hunts Offered

Daily historic tours ($10.00 per adult, children 12 & under $7.00) running every hour and half hour from 9:00 a.m. to 5:00 p.m. Mystery tours are conducted on Friday and Saturday evenings at 6:00, 7:00, and 8:00. The cost is $15.00 per person. Additionally, you may want to reserve a private mystery tour (starting at $200.00).

Price: : Starting at $148.00 per night for Garden Rooms.

Tips & Suggested Itinerary

If you are arriving for a Sunday night stay, the Carriage House Restaurant will be closed for dinner. We grabbed a pizza from Sonny's, which is just down the street from the house.

Closest Airports

Baton Rouge Metropolitan Airport (BTR)—about 27 miles away

Lafayette Regional Airport (LFT)—about 88 miles away

Louis Armstrong New Orleans International Airport (MSY)—
    about 99 miles away

Alexandria International Airport (AEX)—107 miles away

TWO

The Queen Mary
Long Beach, CA

In the late 1980s I saw the Queen Mary as a first-grader. I vaguely remember prodding my parents until they paid to take me on the behind-the-scenes tour. I knew that I was fixated on the first-class swimming pool area, but I could not recall anything more specific about the area or the ship at all, for that matter. Going in to our visit, I knew some of the famous ghost stories, but not much more than that.

History

The ship's maiden voyage was on May 27, 1936, from Southampton to New York City, which took about a week. The ship was the epitome of luxury and class through 1939, carrying British Royalty and the Hollywood elite (think Bob Hope, Ginger Rogers, Fred Astaire, and others). During World War II, the ship was called into service and painted a camouflage gray. This is where the name "The Grey Ghost" came from.

According to the Queen Mary's website, Winston Churchill signed the D-day declaration while on board the ship. An estimated fifteen to sixteen thousand soldiers packed the ship to its gills, and people were sleeping in shifts in just about every available space—including the drained swimming pool! Hitler put a $250,000 price on her head, but no captain could hit her, much less sink her ("Our Story").

The exterior of the Queen Mary.

During the war years, many people died of heat stroke and exhaustion while on board. The temperature below deck was commonly over one hundred degrees, and there was no ventilation or air conditioning. Prisoners of war were held in the forward cargo hold. This was not an area that was built to hold people! The men existed in very extreme conditions, and there is no doubt that many fights broke out that resulted in possible deaths. The official death total is unknown. The ship's archives do not contain information regarding the number of deaths during the war years. The best count is nineteen to twenty crew members and thirty-nine passengers.

There was one major accident that happened on October 2, 1942, when the Queen Mary sliced her escort ship, the HMS Curacoa, in two somewhere across the Irish Sea. There were 439 men on board the Curacoa, and 338 of them perished in the accident. The Curacoa was found at fault for the accident. This incident leads to the biggest theories behind the hauntings on the ship.

The War Years and Burials at Sea

I have another possible theory for all of these hauntings that I have yet to see discussed in print or mentioned in passing. Sometimes passengers and crew members were buried at sea. I find this tradition to be particularly haunting for some reason. It just seems so lonely and unsettled. You can never really know what happens to the body, and no one can ever visit a grave. But there is a purity in it, too. After all, if you are a transient (and aren't we all, if we are brutally honest about it), you are just passing through, wherever you are, and no matter if you have been in the same place for the last twenty years, you are still just a transient on Earth. Exhibits in the ship state that a sailor would traditionally be sewn in his own hammock, but first, a stitch would be made through his nose to make sure he was actually dead. In modern times, wrapping the body in about three yards of canvas at sea would complete the burials; the stitch through the nose was omitted from the customary historic ritual.

I consulted Johnathan Pryor's research paper, "Interment without Earth: A Study of Sea Burials during the Age of Sail," to learn more about handling the dead at sea. Historically, there exists much superstition among sailors from every culture about having a corpse on the ship.

There were important rituals that must be done in order to avoid invoking the anger of the dead. The body had to be washed, dressed, and enshrouded, and then a service had to be held before the body would be committed to the deep. The body would often be weighed down by a cannon ball, shackles, or chains to make sure it would not surface.

Taking into consideration there do not seem to be any records of burials at sea while the Queen Mary was serving as a war ship, it really makes you wonder just how many were thrown over and if there is something to all that superstition after all.

There is a very famous image on file (in the public domain, search identification number "520861") with the National Archives of a burial at sea on board the USS Intrepid after an attack during World War II.

On July 21, 1947, the Queen Mary entered private service once more and reigned supreme through the late 1960s until air travel began to dominate, and it just wasn't profitable to keep her operating in the fleet any longer. When the RMS Queen Mary was retired, the "Last Great Cruise" arrived in Long Beach, California, where she was permanently docked on December 9, 1967, by Captain John Treasure Jones.

Unfortunately, Leonard "Lobster" Horsborough was a cook who died from complications of heat stroke during this last voyage on November 13, 1967. He was buried at sea by his peers.

Visiting the Queen Mary

Bob and I split up and he handled the check-in while I navigated the long hallway to the left of the registration desk. The first thing I noticed was that the hallway seemed to go on forever, and it looked to be wavering back and forth in front of my eyes.

I noticed that about halfway to the public bathroom, the lights grew dimmer, the smell changed to an old hospital smell, and I felt eyes upon me—but no one was around.

A hallway in the Queen Mary.

The ship deck.

The thought that came to me at the time was, "This is going to be an amazing experience. I can smell the dead here."

I would later read that the area where I had this experience was near the forward third-class staircase, which was thought to be the 1936 death site of a little girl. She was sliding down the stair rail when the ship suddenly took a hit from a large wave.

The impact threw her from the rail and caused her to strike her head on the deck. She died instantly of a broken neck.

Bob and I would later talk about all the different and strange old smells we came across amongst our wanderings around the ship and her vast wooden decks. The phrase I coined was "cold wet death."

We had mere moments to spare before meeting the Commodore for our private tour of the ship. Commodore Everette Hoard was interviewed for an article that ran on September 7, 2014, for the Orange County Register.

The reporter asked him if he had ever experienced anything paranormal in his thirty-four years of service on board the ship, and he related an event that happened to him while staying in Suite M-001. Hoard was alone in the room while his wife went to breakfast. He experienced the bed shaking followed by a voice in his ear that said, "I'm cold. I'm so very cold." The Commodore is not certain what ghosts are exactly, but he does believe that the ship is haunted. He described the pull of the ship as a "compelling lure." I agree. It sticks with you for a long time after you leave. The captains believed that the ship was a living, breathing thing. Each man had a bond with her.

The ship is often compared to the Titanic, but the Queen Mary is actually larger. The other difference is that the Titanic was very ornate, while the Queen Mary was tastefully decorated and refined. In fact, it is a small miracle that she was saved and that so many of the original Art Deco details have been preserved. These details are evident in just about every public area that remains open. Some examples include clocks, surrealist paintings, fixtures, and wood paneling details. The first-class dining room had a map, with crystal ships that moved in realtime so that passengers could observe their position in crossing the North Atlantic.

Edward Wadsworth created two of the paintings that can be seen today in the former first-class smoking room. The first is called *Dressed Overall at the Quay* and is arguably more classic and tame than *The Sea*, which was widely criticized as being too surreal for the audience.

If you look closely, you can see an image of the Queen Mary in the background of both paintings.

In viewing and appreciating all of the remaining Art Deco works, I was transported back in time. Every now and then, I will see a place and upon further reflection, grow to appreciate it even more, and the Queen Mary is one of those places. I don't know why, but maybe it has something to do with the romance and luxury of travel in this time period. Now travel is mostly just utility.

The map in the first-class dining room tracked the ship's progress for the passengers.

The first-class dining room.

The Dressed Overall at the Quay *painting by Edward Wadsworth.*

The Sea *painting by Wadsworth.*

The isolation ward of the Queen Mary.

The isolation ward has been preserved and is part of the self-guided tour. In my opinion, this felt like a personal hot spot for lingering paranormal activity. It was not hard to imagine doctors and nurses dressed in 1940s clothing tending to patients in the bunks.

Reports also exist of a "Lady in White" showing herself in this area of the ship (as well as the Queen's salon, where she may be seen sitting alone at a table or dancing by herself).

There were historically five beds in both a female ward and a male ward. It is not clear if anyone died here, although the area was sometimes used to secure stowaways.

I have read that this was the main medical area for any passengers not traveling first class. The Queen Mary did have a separate hospital and surgical theatre for first-class passengers, but these rooms were destroyed long ago.

Sir Winston's restaurant.

Sir Winston's is the fine-dining restaurant on board the ship. The bar area is another famous hot spot where ladies have reported being surprised in the restrooms. That sounds like a very rude and uncultured ghost if you ask me! It is not clear if they are blaming the apparition on Sir Winston Churchill himself, but his spirit has been known to make an appearance from time to time.

One of the other most commonly reported sightings associated with Sir Winston's is a man who wears a top hat and tails. Generally referred to as "the Dude," the figure may walk up behind a guest, clear his throat, and then once the guest turns around to see who is standing behind them, the Dude has pulled a disappearing act. Replicas of the original lifeboats are on display outside the restaurant, and you might be lucky enough to see a demonstration of how they can be lowered.

A replica of an original lifeboat on the Queen Mary.

The officers' quarters.

The bridge and wheelhouse.

Another area where history still hangs in the air is on the Sports Deck. It is here that you can explore the officers' quarters, the bridge, and the wheelhouse. In the ship's early years, there were allegedly a series of deaths on board amongst captains who were nearing retirement. I heard that a captain would never know in their later years when he was making his last journey. The company might tell him just before departure, or they might wait and tell him after he arrived in the port that they were retiring him. That, to me, seems like just about one of the most haunting and traumatic experiences that a worker could go through. You have no time to emotionally and mentally prepare for this major life change. You are just done. It seems like a particularly traumatic experience for a sailor, who would be saying goodbye to the only way of life he knew while at sea. I think that all of this high emotional trauma could be leftover in some form of energy to this day.

The hotel rooms may appear a bit rustic and small to modern luxury travelers, but this is to be expected for a historic property. The bathtub still retained the original handles that guests used to select whether they wanted hot or cold saltwater or freshwater!

A Briefing on Some of the Legends

The Queen Mary has been called one of the most haunted places in the world, and perhaps there is a great deal of truth to that label. Brian Clune and Bob Davis are two paranormal investigators who wrote about the ghostly legends surrounding the ship in their 2014 book entitled *Ghosts of the Queen Mary*. The late Peter James, former resident ship psychic and probably most famous for the television show *Sightings*, thought that he had been in contact with about 600 spirits during the course of his employment on board the ship. Some of the most popular stories that are discussed in *Ghosts of the Queen Mary* could explain some of the following hauntings:

- When the ship was being built in 1934, allegedly two men died and their corpses were later discovered close together, with a welding torch nearby. It is thought that their deaths were caused by poisoned gas. Peter James thought that the spirit called "John Henry" was one of these men.

- There is a spirit of a ghost girl thought to have broken her neck from a slide down the forward third-class banister.

- People have heard sounds of screaming and rushing water in the area of the ship where the propellers used to be. Perhaps this is a residual effect from the Curacoa accident.

- There is a little girl spirit called "Jackie" who may have died in the late 1940s.

- An officer ingested poison and died on the ship. There is an exhibit in the isolation ward that confirms this. William Eric Stark was the officer who died on September 23, 1949, on Voyage 119 West. He was buried at sea. The cause of death was listed as "drank tetrachloride by mistake."

- John Pedder was crushed in a watertight door (Number 13) in 1966 when he was working in the engine room.

I was looking forward to attending Matthew Schulz's ghost hunt later that night, because I knew we would go below deck and get a first-hand chance to explore many of these popular legends.

Evening Ghost Hunt with Matthew Schulz, Project Founder and Investigator—ParaXplorer Project

Matthew Schulz is the RMS Queen Mary's paranormal investigation tour host. He was very kind to meet with me before the official public event began, and I accompanied him on his walk-through and set-up below deck. Due to his flight schedule, Bob was sitting out this late-night event, and I would attend the investigation alone. The evening began at 11:00 p.m. and lasted until well past 3:00 a.m.

Our first stop was in the engine room, and we were briefed on John Pedder and introduced to dowsing rods and some other tools. John Pedder is named within the exhibit on the wall in the isolation ward. His occupation is listed as a fireman, and he died on July 10, 1966, on Voyage 483 West. The cause of death was listed as "crushed in watertight door." John Pedder had only been working about four months when he died. He was just eighteen years old. There was no other evidence to his body that would indicate that he suffered from anything else other than succumbing to a crushing injury. We were allowed to wander for a good deal of time in the area alone or with a small group, and I ventured off by myself to explore and take photos. The lights were kept on (I imagine for insurance reasons), so it was a little difficult to "get in the mood," so to speak. A larger group ahead of me left the area, and I seized the opportunity to try to talk to John. As mentioned, he was just eighteen when he died. Many women have reported that they have interacted with his spirit. Some have even claimed that they have felt phantom touches and the feeling of someone breathing in their ears. While I did not encounter any activity during my few minutes alone in this area, the photo opportunities were incredible, and it was a good experience to be down there without a large crowd or without feeling rushed.

Matthew played some of the class A EVPs that have been captured down here, and what is so amazing to me is that you can hear what sounds like the same male voice responding to different people over the years. I checked back with Matthew, and he clarified that the EVPs appear to come from an older gentleman, possibly an officer saying, "Get out!" and "It restarts me." The EVP possibly attributable to John Pedder was a "Yes" response to the question "Are you here, John?"

Our next stop took us to the boiler room and to the green room, where Matthew had set up an impressive number of experiments. He had laser grids set up for us to sit quietly and watch for shadows to break the light displays. The green room is an area that has some interesting claims associated with it. Clune and Davis wrote about seeing balls of light that were the size of baseballs on three separate investigations. Further, there is a small hole in the ceiling of this room. Witnesses have reported seeing a rugged-looking man staring down at them from this opening. In the main boiler room you can see the catwalks overhead where shadow figures have been known to show themselves.

Matthew also had headsets in the green room that were connected to a recorder with a ten second delay so we could listen to any EVPs captured in real time!

The boiler room.

The pool area.

While I did not personally experience anything while partaking in this part of the ghost hunt, I did note how progressive and thoughtful this outfit was. I have yet to be anywhere where this type of technology is being used during public events. Matthew had quite the setup going on!

The Heart of the Ship

The last area on our hunt was the first-class swimming pool and dressing room. We walked (or scaled, rather) across a dark catwalk to get there. I am struggling with how to write about my feeling and impression of this area without sounding like a melodramatic sap. The best way that I can think of to convey how it felt was that it was as if I had stumbled upon one of those old Hollywood synchronized swimming movies.

The area is extremely dimly lit, and it is hard to make out the colors in the old tile, although they appeared to be a mint green and yellow. While the pool has been drained for structural reasons and is in a state of disrepair, it is evident that the room used to be quite the beauty. The ship supplied some historic photos of the pool.

It feels otherworldly, to say the least, and almost electrically charged. Reports about the pool area range from seeing mysterious wet footprints—remember, the pool has long been drained of all water—all the way to seeing apparitions of women walking around wearing vintage-style bathing suits.

The strangest thing happened here while our entire small group was gathered closely together by the stairs, listening intently while Matthew spoke to "Jackie."

The pool during its heyday.

Jackie is the famous spirit believed to be a little girl that is seen and heard by many visitors to the ship. Clune and Davis wrote that Jackie drowned in the second-class pool area and now frequents the first-class pool area. She is a playful spirit who has been seen by guests playing peekaboo from the stairs and balcony areas of the first-class pool area.

Suddenly, while Matthew was talking, we heard what sounded like the disembodied giggle of a little girl over our heads! I checked back with Matthew to determine if there was any way possible that this could have been a special-effect sound from a tour that coincidentally got tripped at the right time. Matthew responded to my e-mail on April 20, 2015, and confirmed that the Ghosts & Legends Tour that uses special effects had actually been closed down for maintenance since the beginning of 2015. There was no way we could have been hearing lingering special effects from that tour! Further, Matthew stated that sounds such as disembodied little girl giggles and vocalizations were somewhat common experiences on the Queen Mary.

It seems unlikely, given the approximate 2:45 a.m. time, that there would have been an actual child outside the room somewhere making the noise. Additionally, everyone in the group was legitimately shocked to hear this sound. There was no one above us, and I don't believe anyone in the group made this sound. I saw everyone's face and no one looked like they were guilty or having a laugh at everyone else's expense. Matthew also stated that he is a good judge of character from his experiences giving these tours and can usually spot a guest who is trying to pull a trick on the group. I believe it was possible that we were experiencing one of those Direct Voice Phenomenons (DVP—instead of an EVP that is recorded, you actually hear the voice live, without any equipment whatsoever) that Peter James used to report and that Clune and Davis have written about. It was a rare moment for me.

The situation grew more intense when we moved the party to the dressing room. I had a personal experience unlike any I have ever felt before, and it was one of those rare moments that I still have no real explanation for. The feelings I experienced could have been a combination of the pitch darkness, the late hour and how tired I was, and the fear effect; whatever the reason, as we all divided ourselves up and claimed individual changing stalls for our own, I started to get a little bit uneasy. The uneasiness grew to an outright uncomfortable feeling that then spiked to absolute terror. I was alone in the pitch dark but ultimately in close range to a group of people, including our group leader, who had been very nice and accommodating to me, and I trusted him. There were also two nice people directly across from me in their own stall. I could have taken a few steps and reached out and touched other people who had been kind to me earlier in the evening. I have no idea why I started to panic. It makes absolutely no sense. After all, we were in the dark earlier that night when we were investigating in the green room and in the boiler room. I really had to talk myself down in my head. I started to get control of my breathing and I had to keep repeating to myself that I was okay. There was a moment where I felt frozen, and I was afraid to turn around in my stall because I had an image in my mind of a bad lady who had stringy long hair, black eye sockets, and rotting flesh. I rationalized that as long as I refused to acknowledge her existence, she couldn't get me. This is a case of your mind running away from you, because there are no documents of anyone drowning in this pool, and Matthew had not been telling us scary stories in the dark. In fact, he had not even said *anything* about a woman haunting this area at all. Our focus was completely on trying to make contact with Jackie, the child spirit. I was just standing alone in the dark replaying every horror movie I had ever seen on a loop in my own head, like a crazy asshole.

I felt my knees buckle, and I had to steady myself by bracing both arms against the walls. Shortly after that, we all heard a loud knock, seemingly in response to a question, but that could have been anyone on the tour who was further down the hallway in the changing rooms. I got so exhausted and dizzy I began to hallucinate. I thought I was seeing different mist type things at the end of the hallway moving about, but I would blink and shake my head and then there would be nothing but darkness again. I briefly considered curling up in a fetal position at the back of my stall and going to sleep.

I wondered if they would find me, or if I would wake up by myself at 5:30 a.m. in the bowels of the ship and have a heart attack when I realized I was all alone and lost. All of these events cycled through my mind in the course of just a few minutes. Ultimately, I kept chewing on my tongue and reminding myself that I was a badass and needed to get my shit together before somebody had to come and carry me out of there like a little baby. I finished the tour like a champ. When I returned home and began reading about the ship, I found out that many visitors have referred to this area as a vortex or a portal site. In fact, consider these excerpts from *Ghosts of the Queen Mary*:

Page 68: "There are many paranormal hot spots throughout the ship, but as we all know, the first-class poolroom is the center of all the activity that goes on in the ship and is located in the heart of the ship. The corridor of dressing rooms located in the poolroom is rumored to harbor a vortex where the spirits enter and exit, and many psychics believe that a vortex is always located in the heart of a building or location."

Page 112: "This portal to the other side is purported to be located in the narrow aisle between the changing closets, three stalls back from the port side. It is said that if you stand at this spot, you will feel the hair on the back of your neck and on your arms rise, your skin will crawl and eventually you will begin to get dizzy.

People have claimed that when they are near this spot, they get the feeling of being watched, their adrenaline will start to pump uncontrollably and they will have a strong urge to flee the cramped changing room area."

When I came across these passages, I found myself covered in goose bumps from head to toe. Reflecting back upon my ghost adventure while on board the RMS Queen Mary, I am compelled to believe that there is something to all of these claims, because I experienced them firsthand while I was standing in the heart of the ship.

Comments from Bob

It was a great honor to stay on the Queen Mary. While well aware of the historical significance of this ship, I was not aware of the haunted history.

We got about four hours of sleep before driving to Long Beach the day we arrived at the Queen Mary. While I would accompany Jamie around the ship and on the tour by the Commodore, there was no way I would be taking in a late night ghost hunt. Hunting ghosts until 3 a.m. would be Jamie's job.

The tour that Commodore Everette Hoard gave us was exceptional. As I know from flying for a living, if you love what you do, you will never work a day in your life. Commodore Hoard loves the Queen Mary and loves his job. A once aspiring aviator, the Commodore had a great deal of respect for my job and we developed a strong mutual respect during the two hours we were together.

The Commodore was well aware of the haunted history and not only seemed to know the spots that were haunted, he also shared some of his personal experiences. When he took us into the bar area of Sir Winston's, I caught my first sense of the ship feeling haunted.

Jamie used the term "cold wet death" to describe the smells here. Her description is perfect, as I have found a slightly modified version that I have come to recognize in haunted places. My term, "cold, wet, *clammy* death," seems to come closer. Most of the haunted places I have been seem to give me a perceptible, although sometimes barely perceptible, feeling and odor of cold, wet, and clammy death. The Piano Bar had that feel and I recognized it the minute we walked into the room. I am not sure whether this feeling and odor causes the hairs to stand up on my neck or whether the standing hairs are a natural by-product of the cold, wet, clammy death, but the two go hand in hand.

Whoever or whatever was in Sir Winston's Bar probably was a soul who had his or her vices in life and still resonates with the activities that went on in that particular room. I wish I could have bought him a glass of wine, or at least a ticket home.

If You Decide to Visit

Location & Contact Info

1126 Queens Highway

Long Beach, CA 90802

Tel: 877-342-0742

E-mail: *reservations@queenmary.com*

Website: *http://www.queenmary.com*

Type of Tours & Hunts Offered

So many! During daylight hours book a Haunted Encounters Tour. After dark, they offer twilight tours, séances, a special dining program, and investigations.

Size: 346 original staterooms on 3 decks

Price: Starting at $149.00 per night for standard Staterooms

Closest Airports

Los Angeles International Airport (LAX)—about 22 miles away

San Diego International Airport (SAN)—about 106 miles away

Palm Springs International Airport (PSP)—about 118 miles away

THREE

The Copper Queen Hotel
Bisbee, AZ

Bisbee is weird. A T-shirt in a shop in town told me so. The message read: "Keep Bisbee weird." We've been there twice, and both times it's felt as though we have stepped into a different plane of reality. To me, the entire historic district feels haunted. While walking one afternoon, we saw a bumper sticker that declared, "Bisbee, AZ. It's like Mayberry on acid." Yep. There is an artist culture in residence that contributes to a freethinking-free spirit-anything goes type of vibe.

The first time we came to town it was New Year's Day. Before I had read anything about the town, Bob and I were taking a walk around historic downtown when I looked over at him and said, "Something bad happened here. Something is really not right here." I later inadvertently walked into the path of a fantastic female drunk outside a bar in the main section of town.

The exterior of the Copper Queen Hotel.

She was absolutely losing her mind and screaming loud enough in some mix of English and Spanish to wake the devil, although I can't exactly be sure what language she was speaking (or attempting to speak). It actually bore no resemblance to any language I have ever heard. I stood frozen for a few seconds when her eyes locked with mine.

There was no need to worry, though, as she was deliriously and dangerously drunk, and she never saw me even though we were looking right at each other. I took in the scene for a few seconds more. I considered helping her for a moment, but then my instincts kicked in and I remained true to my Southern roots. I did what any self-respecting Southerner would do in the same situation: I turned and walked away. It has never benefited me (or the other adult person, for that matter) when I have inserted myself into another person's business. That's Bisbee, as the locals say.

The second time we saw Bisbee, I fought the urge to hold my breath and make a wish when we entered the Mule Pass Tunnel. We needed some exercise after our drive, so we began walking some of the stairs that are listed on the Bisbee 1000 stair climb—these concrete stairs that snake up and down the hillsides of Bisbee came about in the 1930s when Mr. Roosevelt tried to save us all with the WPA. We were walking the stairs when we encountered a human zombie. When we first saw him, we initially waved and said hello.

It wasn't until he got closer to us that we realized he resembled a cast member of AMC's *The Walking Dead*. Bob guessed he was a heroin addict, but he looked like a brain-eating zombie to me.

That's Bisbee. We were nearly running back down the stairs to get back to the "safe" main road where all the shops are in town. To this day, no mail service delivers to the homes, and Bisbeeites must walk down to the post office to pick up their mail.

We briefly met the Duchess of Hemp at her restaurant (the Stock Exchange Saloon). She is a retired lobbyist from Washington, D.C. and is quite charming and entertaining. The pizza was good too.

We observed another interesting exchange between a local woman and her husband. He was urging her to stop talking because "We have to get home before dark." I wondered if the zombies got worse after dark. That's Bisbee.

But I digress. Back to trying to get the pulse on the weirdness. One local over at *bisbeeblog.com* writes that when he first moved to town from Key West, he thought the weirdness must come from something in the water, but he's been told that it is a "combination of crystals and ley lines." I can buy that.

Downtown Bisbee.

On March 21, 2006, *Budget Travel* magazine included Bisbee in their roundup article of "The Coolest Small Towns in the U.S.A." The article quoted resident Cynthia Conroy as saying: "Bisbee is for people who don't like the ordinary." This is evident as you stroll the streets and see public displays of art. There are no cookie cutter subdivisions in Bisbee. You will see houses painted any variety of colors, you will see people sleeping in vans randomly parked on side streets and in yards or parking lots, and you will see car doors that are now serving as front gates.

I also believe there is something to the stone tape theory regarding the geology and mining continuing to affect mining towns. Bisbee and Jerome both feel as though you are one large clap of lightning away from either being transported back in time or the past being transported to the present and catching up with you. According to the Bisbee Mining and Historical Museum, Bisbee has an estimated 2,200 miles of tunnels. The comparison given at the museum is that one could essentially travel from Portland to Chicago without seeing the light of day. Think about this little tidbit on the museum's website: "In fact, many local homes and businesses come complete with their own subterranean passageways" ("Welcome to Bisbee"). In my mind, the scariest thing about Bisbee is the fact that we just don't know who or what is walking around underground. What if there is a passage or multiple passages underneath Bisbee that leads to a secret ancient society underground? There are many historical stories about explorers who have wandered off underground, never to be heard from again. What if they wandered into another world?

Inside the mining museum, there is a picture from November 12, 1897, of the Freemasons from the Masonic Grand Lodge of Arizona who apparently decided to hold their meetings somewhere inside a cave deep in the Mule Mountains. Think about how creepy that is for a second. I'll wait for you.

History

Ethel Jackson Price wrote in her introduction to *Bisbee: Images of America* that few white men went over the Mule Mountains until the late 1870s because most people who did so disappeared. She does not speculate about the cause of the disappearance. It sounds as though Bisbee has always been strange and unusual. Richard Shelton points out in *Going Back to Bisbee* that there are an unknown amount of unidentified graves and murders throughout the area because of the history of ranching and the historically exploitative relationships between the ranchers and the workers, the Apaches (their victims were unknown because oftentimes mutilation made identification impossible), and the drug activity so close to the border.

Bisbee was a copper (but also gold and silver) mining town founded in 1880, and it is situated amongst the Mule Mountains just eight miles from the border of Mexico.

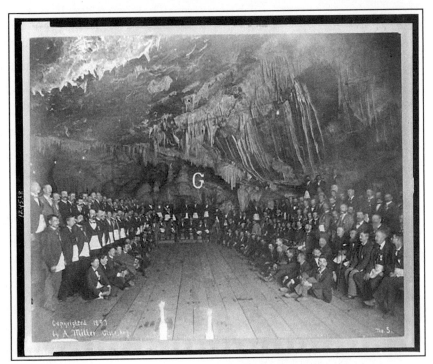

The November 12, 1897, meeting of the local Freemasons took place in its usual spot: a cave in the Mule Mountains.

Lynn Bailey points out in *Bisbee: Queen of the Copper Camps* that the Mule Mountains are comprised of carboniferous limestone, naco limestone, escabrosa limestone, and Martin limestone. Limestone is thought to be a natural conductor of residual paranormal occurrences.

Nearly all writings I have come across about Bisbee describe the town as being "nestled" in the Mule Mountains. I disagree. That word implies that Bisbee is sheltered and protected by the mountains. My impression is that Bisbee exists in spite of these mountains, and not because of them. There is no nestling. There is no "safe." Bisbee is situated.

At one point in the early 1900s, the population was around twenty thousand and the town thrived. Ethel Price reported that the main street of the town saw sweeping, devastating fires in 1879 (or 1880), 1890, 1896,

1902, and the summer of 1908 (or 1910). Price also mentioned the destructive summer monsoons that would plague the town, but she said that there were only two deaths caused by the floods—two miners that drowned in their home. Richard Shelton wrote that between 1888 and 1900, hundreds of citizens died because of typhoid, smallpox, and diphtheria.

Perhaps the biggest blight on Bisbee was the Bisbee Deportation of July 12, 1917, when the largest mass kidnapping in America occurred. Half of the mine workers had been on strike since June 24.

It is estimated that a thousand men were rounded up by a vigilante group hired by the copper companies and forced onto trains that brought them to New Mexico. Families were pulled apart and many of the men never returned home.

President Woodrow Wilson led a commission to investigate the deportation, but no action was ever taken against the copper companies for this atrocious act. I believe that this is what I was sensing in the air upon my first visit to Bisbee when I said out of nowhere, "something bad happened here." I think this was such an emotional and traumatic event that it left an imprint on the land.

By the 1950s, the town population had dwindled to approximately six thousand, and by 1975, Phelps Dodge closed their mines. Just like in Jerome, Arizona, artists and hippies moved in and took advantage of rock bottom housing prices. Bob and I are not the only ones to have an ominous feeling about Bisbee.

Jill Pascoe, author of *Arizona's Haunted History*, wrote about her impression of Bisbee: "There is a forlorn sense, a feeling of loss even with all the bright facades," (191). She too theorizes that it has to do with the history of tragedy on the land. Richard Shelton wrote that even in 1958, "There was a general feeling of abandonment, of dying, and a lack of energy in the air" (283). Bob and I think the whole damn town is haunted.

The Old Bisbee Ghost Tour

We booked the Old Bisbee Ghost Tour with Renée, who is also the author of *Southern Arizona's Most Haunted*, and she runs ghost hunts at the Copper Queen Hotel as well. At 7:00 p.m. we met our "Ghost Host" on the stairs in front of the Bisbee Mining and Historical Museum. Renée was very informative and briefed us about many of the legends surrounding the haunted hotels in Bisbee. She probably spent about two hours with our small group, and we did not get bothered or interrupted by anyone while on our tour. Our after-dark experience was surprisingly peaceful. We saw the Bisbee Grand Hotel, the Oliver House, and were even able to go inside and walk around inside the Bisbee Inn. I remember thinking that there are *a lot* of stories of paranormal events for such a small area—the historic district is only about two miles of the town!

Oliver House Legends

There are three big legends associated with the Oliver House. The first legend counts the death toll at twenty-seven people since 1908, and this is probably the main reason attributed to the hauntings. The second legend is that a man by the name of Nat Anderson was murdered here on February 22, 1920. The third legend dates to 1932 when a local police officer shot his wife and the man he discovered her cheating with in the home, and then he shot himself.

The legend surrounding Nat Anderson appears to be rooted in cold hard facts. There is a death certificate on file with the Arizona Department of Health Services for Nat Anderson from February 22, 1920. Renée actually showed us a copy of Nat's death certificate during her tour. The cause of death was listed as gunshot wound (pistol) in forehead, and the official report states that he died in the Copper Queen Hospital, and not at a private address. A February 29, 1920, newspaper article titled "Murder of Anderson Baffles the Police" from the *Tombstone Epitaph* reported that Nat was a roadmaster for the Copper Queen Company and was rooming at the Oliver House. Kay Ross, another boarder and timekeeper at the Sacramento mine, discovered that his room had been robbed. Initially, investigators thought that the man responsible for the Ross robbery killed Anderson. However, given the following details about the murder, it was concluded that the robbery was not likely to have been connected with Anderson's death. The article read:

> The way in which Anderson was shot points to a personal grudge on the part of his assailant rather than the work of a man who was desperately trying to get away. The first bullet struck him in the forehead and was probably sufficient to cause his death. As he fell, a second bullet coursed down his breast, making a flesh wound without entering the body. Then, as the man lay prone on his face his assailant deliberately fired a third bullet into the lower part of his back. Nat Anderson died Sunday afternoon at 1:30 without ever having regained consciousness.

The sitting area of the lobby.

The Copper Queen

The fifty-two-room hotel was opened in 1902 by Phelps Dodge to serve the luxury lodging needs of their executives. At some point, the building served as a triage hospital. I chose the Julia Lowell Suite for our room. The Suite is advertised on the hotel website by suggesting guests should "Spend the night with our lady of the evening. Watch the sultry dance of her spirit or allow her to rub your feet as you sleep. This room was the business center for one of our most famous guests in the property, Julia Lowell. This room with a queen bed is decorated in a bordello fashion just the way she would have had it."

We did some hanging out in the public areas of the Copper Queen to try and get a feel for the place. I couldn't help but think of *The Shining* when I saw an old fire hose in the wall.

The hotel itself is a creepy old place. It looks creepy on the outside and the air is heavy on the inside. The Julia Lowell suite has an antique vibe, and you cannot help but notice the historic license for prostitution that is hung on the wall. No, this was not Julia's actual license.

It is important to note that room 315 has been set aside in Julia's honor, but it is not known if this is the room that Julia actually died in. I was unable to locate a death certificate for Julia Lowell.

The Arizona Department of Health Services has birth and death certificates that are searchable online; the only birth and death for a person in Cochise County named "Julia" is for an infant who died of dysentery in 1931. The story told about Julia Lowell reminds me of the classic vanishing hitchhiker or "lady in white" stories that seem to circulate in every town. There very well may have been a prostitute who killed herself inside the hotel. I just don't think her name was Julia Lowell. There are several murders and deaths mentioned throughout *Bisbee: Queen of the Copper Camps*. The subject of prostitution is covered in much detail in chapter 8, and Bailey lists a few notorious prostitutes in the book, but none are Julia Lowell and none of the stories contain any mention of suicide and death.

The tin ceiling of the dining area of the hotel.

The stairwell in the lobby.

The Julia Lowell suite.

For your quick reference, Bailey lists some of the usual suspects, which include: Clara Allen, Frida Miller, Hilda Miller, Rozelia Castilla, Black Fanny (this is my nominee for best prostitute name), Grace Martin, Birdie Russell, Mrs. Bell Hunter, Ethel Sheriff, and Mrs. Mary A. Bacon.

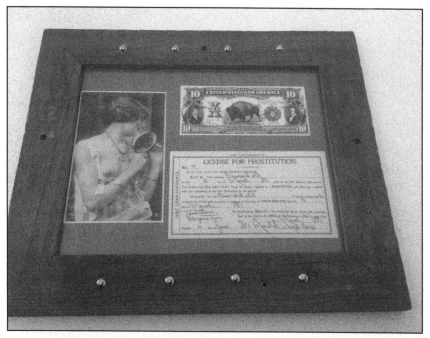
A license for prostitution is framed and located in Julia's suite.

The ghost lore at the hotel is so extensive that the guest book entries left by visitors were turned into a book entitled *The Ghosts of The Copper Queen Hotel*. The book spans from 2000 to 2008, and there are numerous entries specific to the Julia Lowell room, including reports from guests claiming that they have actually seen her spirit (a full-body apparition).

Other notable claims related to the legend of Julia include women who stay in the room and report feelings of oppression or of being unwelcome, men who are touched in the night or people who have covers moved from the bed, and phantom cheap perfume smells. There are thought to be at least sixteen spirits at the Copper Queen.

According to an interview found on YouTube with Stephen Hudson, the night auditor, the main story is that Julia was a lady of negotiable affection (this is a nice way of calling her a prostitute) who lived at the hotel in the 1920s. Her father owned the hotel, and he built her a walkway up to the third floor to keep foot traffic away from the main door. She fell in love with one of her customers, and when he did not reciprocate her feelings, she committed suicide somewhere in the hotel.

Another legendary character has come to be called "Billy." He is thought to have been an eight- or nine-year-old boy who had a family member either working or living at the hotel. He died in the San Pedro River and is believed to have traveled back to the hotel looking for his family member.

In *Southern Arizona's Most Haunted*, Billy is reported as the most playful spirit at the hotel, and he has been held responsible for items moved around guest rooms, including candy taken with wrappers left behind, laughing throughout the hallways of the hotel, and jumping on furniture. Of the stories that Renée relates, the one I find the most compelling is the report from a little girl in the dining room who told her parents, after being asked what she kept doing during dinner, that she was playing with a little boy under the table. Renée also wrote that the local lore is that Julia Lowell hung herself. Apparently, the reports are that she is still working at the Copper Queen trying to seduce men, even in death.

One of the hotel's front desk employees told us when we were leaving that she's experienced an unexplainable smell of phantom cigar smoke throughout the hotel. Given the extensive reports of haunted occurrences at the Copper Queen Hotel, I was curious what other local paranormal investigation teams had currently been experiencing. Here are a few of their firsthand accounts.

Becky Gydesen—Owner of Tucson Ghost Company, LLC and Founder and Lead Investigator of the Tucson Ghost Society

My husband and I stayed at the Copper Queen back in December 2014 in Julia's room. Being a paranormal investigator, I often try to get to haunted places and do my own investigation. We set up DVR cameras, a Rem Pod, and left a recorder going and left the room after checking in to go explore.

When playing back the EVPs when we got back to the hotel, we could hear the Rem Pod going off and strange noises in the room like little knocking sounds and movement. We decided to explore some and went up toward Billy's room, but it was rented so we couldn't go in. I did invite him to come down to Julia's room and we did get some EVPs that sounded like it could be a boy, but they were not audible.

We still have to listen to the full nights EVPs, but I can tell you during the night our K-II kept going off and so did the Rem Pod. I also had a freezing cold spot by my ankles that stayed from about my ankles to my knee area; even my husband, Will, could feel the difference in the temperature around that area. When we were in bed we felt a tug at the blankets. My husband felt the sensation of his feet being played with, and in the morning he could feel someone sit on the bed next to him. Also my phone got played with because no one was near it, but Siri came on. I had been asking Julia a question and you hear Siri repeating my question. Needless to say we didn't get a lot of sleep because we left the equipment on all night, and Julia seemed to love making that Rem Pod go off every time we were ready to doze off!

Vincent Amico—Lead Investigator, AZ Paranormal Investigation & Research Society

We did a casual investigation at the Copper Queen a few years back as it was really a quick getaway trip. Nothing official, as we prefer minimal people around, and this visit was Memorial Day weekend and there were people everywhere.

I stayed in Billy's room and did have good responses to questions using a K-II, but with all the activity at the hotel we ruled it out as possible radio frequency interference (RFI) from cell phones.

Two other investigators sitting away from where the K-II was positioned had no fluctuations on their Mel Meters during the activity with the K-II. We did have solid lights lit for a couple of seconds each time when we asked for a response. (With RFI you get more pulsing lights bouncing between 1.5 mG and 10 mG.) We still ruled it out as K-II are very susceptible to interference and it could have been multiple cell phone use causing steady lights.

We did set up toys and fake jewelry on the desk and had a camcorder set on it all night. When my wife and I woke, we checked and found many pieces were out of position. When I checked the camcorder, oddly enough, it was powered down. It was plugged in so it was not battery failure and it has a thirty-gig hard drive with plenty of room. We used these cameras many times before and they never shut off. It wasn't a thermal shutdown, as it was in the low seventies in the room according to the Mel Meter readings. The only thing I can conclude is possibly a voltage anomaly in the AC and it shut down. Upon review of the three hours that was recorded, there was no evidence of any movement.

We got an EVP in Billy's room but for me the "too young" is too clear with too much variation in tone and pitch. Since the walls are thin, someone could have heard the question and responded from the hallway, yet none of us heard anything at that moment. Our tech guy Jerry disagrees as it does sound like a young boy's voice and it was late at night and unlikely a child was in the hallway. Jerry stayed in Julia's room and he ran a recorder during the night and we caught what sounds like "I love you." Even that could have been someone in the next room saying "I love you" to who they were with.

Interesting weekend and with what we caught, most paranormal teams would be pumping their fists in delight. I am still skeptical and I consider everything inconclusive since there are rational explanations for most occurrences that night. The only unexplained thing was the items on the desk that moved during the night. Without video footage, there is no proof as before and after photos are useless. It could be said an investigator moved those items before the final picture was taken, so it would not be valid evidence.

I'd love to go back and do it right in a controlled situation.

Mable Jordan—Southern Arizona Spirit Seekers

We stayed at the Copper Queen Hotel in room 210. The first thing that happened was the draining of our batteries. A charm was slapped out of my hand and flew to the left down the sink. The TV went on and off by itself. There were conversations overheard in our room that night that sounded as though the voices were fighting and someone was throwing things. We also heard scratching noises on the wall and dragging noises throughout the night. Someone jumped on our bed. My husband woke up to someone caressing his hand two times. I can't wait to go back. It was a wild night!

Fernando Villa—The Border Paranormal Society

I lived and worked at the Copper Queen Hotel as an assistant manager in 1992. In fact, I stayed in what is now known as Julia's Room for about a month. At this time, the legend about Julia wasn't being circulated. I never had any experiences in this room. However, I did have an experience in the middle of the first floor hallway leading to my room (#211) that I can't explain.

As I was walking toward my room, I distinctly heard the elevator door open right behind me and a couple (male and female) emerge. I could hear their soft murmuring as well as the pounding of their footfalls on the carpeted hallway. I could also make out the rustling of clothes against the walls as they moved across the hallway. Just as they began to get very close to me I—as a courtesy—moved out of the way to let them go by—since they appeared to be in a hurry to get to their room—only to find the hallway completely empty and devoid of any sound or living person. Now, except for one other occupied room, the hotel was completely empty at the time, and I did check with the front desk to see if anybody had just checked in, but was informed that no one had.

Overnight at the Copper Queen

Despite my attempts to make contact with anyone that night in the Julia Lowell Suite, the flashlights would not light up. We went to bed with some cash laid out on the nightstand as bait. We woke up and nothing was amiss or out of order in the room. If Julia tickled Bob's toes in the night, he slept right through it and so did I.

We did not witness any strange activity or smell any phantom scents whatsoever during our stay. My instinct on the phantom perfume smells would be to say that it has something to do with cleaning products or that it is simply attributable to live guests with poor taste.

Despite having no personal experiences to report, oddly enough, we both woke up and told each other about the dreams that we had during the night. We were drowning. Yes, both of us dreamed that we were drowning. In my dream, I was totally calm, but I was aware of the fact that I was being swept away by very fast brown water. I don't know if it was a river or what it was. I just remember being carried away by the water. I was fine. I wasn't fighting—I just let the water take me away. Did Billy come to us in our dreams?

Or is the more likely explanation that the dreams were caused by the fresh stories we heard just a few hours before on *Renée*'s tour? We heard a lot of stories on the tour, though, and we heard a lot about different characters, places, and circumstances.

We found it strange that this one story would stick with both of us and haunt our dreams while staying in the hotel. It would seem less strange to us, for instance, if Bob had dreamed about drowning, and I dreamed about seeing a man walking down the hall dressed in a top hat.

To have the same dream was strange. You know what they say, I guess. That's Bisbee.

Comments from Bob

Maybe it is the geology and all the minerals in the rocks that give mining towns like Bisbee, Arizona, a haunted feel. The underground minerals seem to hold, conduct, and transmit energy, and we believe the soul has energy. The town of Bisbee seems to vibrate with a very powerful residual energy.

Like Jamie and those she quoted said, Bisbee has a forlorn feel to it. I cannot compete with how Jamie put it—how it is situated rather than nestled. Because of the way the town is situated, it never receives direct sunlight, at least in January when we were there, so that might also contribute to how it feels.

I tend to shy away from studying the folklore stories of haunted places, so I will leave those stories to others. I prefer to sense, face-to-face, each town and hotel we visit to see if my senses and intuitions pick up anything. I don't want the power of suggestion to skew the mental pictures all six of my senses are picking up.

Walking in Bisbee and sitting in the Copper Queen, one can still feel the ethereal echoes of a thriving, entrepreneurial, blue-collar town. The feelings of determination and grit are still residually palpable, but they seem anathema to the hippie culture that has crashed there. The energies seem to compete as old versus new America.

On the one hand, there is the "this is what makes America the land of opportunity" sense, with a can-do attitude that dug thousands of miles of mining tunnels through solid rock and provided much needed copper to a growing, thriving America. That spirit seems to clash with the "the biggest problem in America today is the inability to buy legal marijuana" spirit that is modern-day Bisbee.

Aside from the residual feel of Bisbee, the active hauntings I sensed here involved the people we encountered. Most were friendly, but I got the sense that the town that outsiders never get to see is living the movie *Beetlejuice* with Michael Keaton's character, Betelgeuse, raising hell all over the place. In fact, that might be the most logical explanation for why Bisbee feels the way it does. Beetlejuice on drugs.

If You Decide to Visit

Location & Contact Info

11 Howell Ave.

Bisbee, Arizona 85603

Tel: 520-432-2216

E-mail: *info@copperqueen.com*

Website: *http://www.copperqueen.com*

Type of Tours & Hunts Offered

The Old Bisbee Ghost Tour: Thursday–Friday, $15.00 per adult. They also currently run ghost hunts for guests only on every first and third Thursday night. Tour info: *http://www.oldbisbeeghosttour.com/*

Size: 52 rooms

Price: Rooms can be booked for under $100.

Tips & Suggested Itinerary

The Queen Mine Tour and the Bisbee Mining & Historical Museum are both world-class stops that are not to be missed. The Queen Mine Tour takes guests 1,500 feet into the mine! The mining museum is the first museum in the southwest to be designated a Smithsonian Affiliate.

Closest Airports

Tucson International Airport (TUS)—about 90 miles away

Phoenix Sky Harbor International Airport (PHX)—
about 206 miles away

FOUR

The Kehoe House
Savannah, GA

Savannah has been named one of America's most haunted cities by *USA Today*. Port cities often have rich haunted histories. Maybe the proximity to the water serves as a conduit for spiritual energy. In 1733, James Oglethorpe obtained permission from Yamacraw chief Tomochichi to build Savannah (GeorgiaInfo). Savannah's history also includes voodoo, pirates, wars, natural disasters, and many deaths from disease. The Creek Indians were living and dying in what is now known as Savannah over 2,500 years ago. The Savannah Historic District is comprised of more than twenty squares that contain museums, shops, galleries, parks, and mansions. The area is the largest National Historic Landmark in the country.

In its early days, Savannah had a few terrible fires that ravaged the historic downtown and riverfront areas. The yellow fever epidemic of 1820 has a conservative death toll estimated to be at around 660.

The exterior of the Kehoe House.

As the city grew, it built upon its dead. Houses and commercial buildings were constructed right over burial grounds, and numerous tour guides have told us that when people renovate, it is routine to find human remains in the ground. Tour guides also report that Chatham County's local courts ruled in the 1950s that having a ghost in your house is a structural defect, and sellers must list paranormal activity in their disclosure statements. With so much haunted history, it seems as though you could pick any building and find stories that claim it's haunted! Still, there was something about the attic windows at the top of the Kehoe House that attracted me at first glance. I had the sense that someone or something was up there looking down at us each time we walked past the house on our evening jaunts. Soon I would get the chance to explore my hunch.

History

William Kehoe was an Irish immigrant and when he came to America in 1851, he was nine years old and his family had nothing. By 1877 he was working as a foreman at an iron foundry by the name of Phoenix. When the owner died in 1878, he left the foundry to his wife and also to William Kehoe. Mr. Kehoe worked for two years until he was able to buy the widow's share of the business and establish Kehoe Iron Works.

The five-story Renaissance Revival Kehoe House was designed by DeWitt Bruyn and built in 1892. William Kehoe's granddaughter, Anne Ritzert, wrote a biography article for the *Savannah News-Press Magazine* in 1969 that described him as a hard-working, religious, and charitable family man (he did have ten children) who also cared about his employees at the iron foundry. His theory on success was, "not wealth for status but wealth for comfortable living, broadening travel and culture, if you enjoyed it" (Ritzert). I like the sound of that.

After his wife Anne Flood passed away and his children were adults, Mr. Kehoe sold the home. Kehoe Iron Works went bankrupt during the Great Depression.

We know from tax records that the home served as a mortuary as early as 1937. From the 1950s to the 1970s, the home was owned by Goette Funeral Home. The basement area of the home contained the embalming room, and the two front rooms of the house were viewing rooms. There were also viewing rooms in the two front rooms on the second floor. In 1955, Goette was desperate for parking and wanted to raze the home next door, the 1820 Davenport House, which drove seven local women into forming the Historic Savannah Foundation. The Foundation has restored and saved over 350 buildings in town.

Football legend Joe Namath and business partner James Walsh bought the home in 1980 for $80,000 and sold it in 1990 for $530,000. The property has served as an upscale bed and breakfast since 2002.

The dining room of the Kehoe House.

Visiting the Kehoe House

We checked in to the Kehoe House on a Tuesday evening in October. As we walked up to the house at dusk and saw the mansion reigning supreme over Columbia Square in historic downtown Savannah, the house appeared to be a beautiful, happy home. I immediately recalled a quote from Bill Bryson's *The Lost Continent.* Upon seeing Savannah for the first time, Bryson wrote, "I did not know that such perfection existed in America." It does, and we get to live it every day.

The home itself was warm, welcoming, and full of countless valuable antiques. Currently there is a wine and cheese reception every evening from 5:00 to 7:00 p.m. in the front room, and breakfast begins at 7:30 a.m. Meals are served in "the viewing room."

Yes, this is a carryover from the old Goette Funeral Home days. Some believe that a former funeral home can leave residual sad energy in a building. This might be true, but I did not have any feelings one way or the other. In fact, if I had not known it was a former funeral home, I would never have guessed it based off appearance. It felt like an upscale bed and breakfast destination.

A bellman took us upstairs to our room, and when asked about his paranormal experiences, he told me that he had not personally experienced anything in the home. However, one of his coworkers informed him when he started his new job that "It's not haunted. There are two children, and they live here. This is their house."

Bob and I embarked on a few local ghost tours to find out what the local guides had to say about the hauntings at the Kehoe House. The first tour we went on claimed that two of the rambunctious Kehoe boys perished in a tragic bonfire around the new year.

The stairway leading to the guest rooms.

This version of the story recounted a tale of a block party in one of Savannah's squares on New Year's Eve. Apparently, the different neighborhoods would compete to see who could build the biggest bonfire. The story goes that two of the Kehoe teenagers perished from a fire that raged out of control. There is also a tale of a mysterious woman in white who is seen in some of the bedrooms.

Our next tour claimed that the Kehoe House had spirits of children playing on the third floor, and the guide believed that it was the grown Kehoe descendants returning to their happy childhood home in death and "living" again as children during their happiest times. At night, guests have heard the sounds of giggling children accompanied by the sounds of running feet. Some have claimed that they have been awakened in the night by a child pulling their bedcovers down. It is important to note that the Kehoe House is an adults-only hotel. If you hear a child giggling, it is not coming from a real child!

There are many stories on the Internet and even in books that tell the tale of the twin Kehoe girls who perished in the home while playing in the chimney. The most elaborate story I have heard about the death of a child in the Kehoe House came from a tour guide. They claimed it was actually the youngest female who was discovered dead within the chimney of the home. The guide attributed the death to a game of hide-and-go-seek gone awry. In his version of the tale, Mr. Kehoe was being a good sport and playing hide-and-go-seek with his youngest daughter, when he was suddenly called away to an emergency at work. It was a sweltering summer day in Savannah.

When he returned home that evening, his youngest daughter was not at the dinner table, and the family did not know where she was. They interrupted dinner to look for the missing daughter, but despite their best efforts, she could not be located. When Mr. Kehoe sought help from the police, their 48-hour investigation did not result in any leads.

The commemorative detail in the chimney.

After exhausting all investigative efforts to locate the missing girl, the police chief told Mr. Kehoe that he thought he had a kidnapping situation on his hands, and he directed him to go home and wait for the ransom demand. Mr. Kehoe returned home, and he sat and waited as another summer day in Savannah heated up around him. As the day wore on, there was an undeniable smell that he recognized. He followed the smell of death and was led to the chimney.

With a sinking feeling of devastation, he looked up and found the decaying body of his youngest daughter. Her nightgown had trapped her in the chimney while climbing up it and trying to win the hide-and-go-seek game with her father. There is a commemorative decoration in the chimneys on the main floor that all the guides claim was put there in remembrance of the child's death.

In Al Cobb's *Savannah's Ghosts*, he interviewed a tour guide by the name of Mitchell Mayer, who claimed that on two different occasions he had young girls on his tour stare up at the Kehoe House attic. The girls said they were looking at a little girl dressed in a white dress who was smiling at them.

In *Haunted Savannah*, James Caskey relays stories about guests who stayed in rooms 201 and 203. The guest in 201 woke up in the middle of the night "after feeling someone softly stroking her hair and cheek," and when she opened her eyes, she saw a young child, who then completely vanished. Another woman staying in room 203 woke up feeling as though someone was next to her in the room. Caskey also reports occurrences of staff hearing doorbells ringing on their own and then doors being opened by themselves as though the person on the other side was tired of being kept waiting!

I wanted to know if there was any truth to the story of twin girls (or one child, for that matter) dying within the chimney of the home. I located a Kehoe descendant who was kind enough to participate in an interview. Below is her story that explains her understanding of the history of the home.

The Story as Told by Tara Kehoe Ryan, Great-Great-Granddaughter of William Kehoe

I spoke with Tara on October 26, 2013. She owns her own tour company, Tara Tours, and while she has never lived in the home, she has been welcomed as an overnight guest on countless occasions.

Some of her personal experiences include hearing children whispering and giggling when she has been trying to sleep. She has also walked into what felt like a sliding glass door in the middle of one of the rooms. A reputable psychic told her that feeling was caused by her great-grandmother, Anne Flood, letting her know that she is still there.

I asked Tara to shed some light on the rumors about the home. She did confirm that two of the Kehoe girls passed away in the home at very young ages, but they succumbed to roseola and passed within days of each other—not while playing in the chimneys. They weren't twins, but they strongly resembled each other and were only two years apart. Anna Louise Kehoe passed away on September 19, 1902, and was four years old. Mary Elizabeth Kehoe was almost two years old when she passed right after her sister on September 22, 1902. The girls died on the third floor of the house, but their spirits are believed to be everywhere throughout the home. Tara told me, "These beautiful blonde hair, blue-eyed angels are extremely playful all throughout the home."

Additionally, one of the original ten Kehoe children, Francis Percy Kehoe, died in the home at the age of forty-one of tuberculosis. Matriarch Anne Flood is believed to be the mysterious woman in white. She died at the age of seventy-three in the Tybee Room on the second floor. She had severe rheumatoid arthritis.

Tara has felt a sadness in certain rooms of the home, and she believes that this is residual energy left over from when the Kehoe House was used as a funeral home. She believes that some of her relatives remain in the Kehoe House in spirit form because it was a happy place for them. Perhaps the girls still continue to play and be happy children in their home.

Evening Sets In at the Kehoe House

We were given nearly full access to the home (all guests are), and we wandered along the creaking wooden floors going from room to room and exploring. Nothing in particular was resonating with me during our walk. We climbed the massive cantilever stairs all the way to the loft attic area. As soon as we entered the room the smell of old wood and historic building materials overcame me. Jackpot!

The attic area of the Kehoe House.

I love it when I can smell history, and I became fascinated with the room immediately. There are exposed wooden beams and pipes up here that I believe were radiating the old smell (there were also some sections of exposed brick). There are two beautiful large windows up here, on the front and on the back of the home, that overlook the city.

To me, this picture gives the impression that you are standing inside a painting, looking out at the world. I felt so happy and safe up here in this loft.

I was really enjoying the pitter-patter from the rain that was coming down that night. I let the sound lull me into a deep state of coziness and well-being. I pretended that I was home. I had heard that Mr. Kehoe's favorite area of the home was also up in the loft. From the front window, he could see his iron foundry and his old Irish neighborhood. He could enjoy his retreat while also keeping a close eye on things. When I was later telling Tara about being drawn to the loft, she confirmed that this was indeed William Kehoe's favorite spot to look over Savannah, and that he loved to be up there for thunderstorms! Sometimes he would use it to hold private business meetings, and he even used the space to provide housing to some of his fellow Irish immigrants. The tiny wooden stairs that lead all the way to the roof still remain, although access to the roof is blocked.

Bob and I walked around the attic for about fifteen minutes taking it all in. We decided to do a flashlight session, and we immediately started getting some activity. I began the session by introducing ourselves and explaining how the flashlights work by twisting the top to produce light.

I said that we had heard many stories that a child, or possibly two Kehoe children, had died in the chimney of the home. I then asked if there were any children with us that night and stood in silence and waited for a response. About thirty to forty seconds later, one of the flashlights emitted a very brief and very low-powered light flash. I thanked whoever it was for the response and asked them to turn the light back down so I could continue trying to speak with them.

When something like this first happens, I usually remember to state that I cannot see them or hear them and that for whatever reason that might be, the flashlights are the best way for us to communicate. I spent the next few minutes trying to talk to whoever else might be with us into turning the light all the way off.

The flashlight was still on the floor where I had left it, giving off a very faint light. Finally after about seven to nine minutes, I said, "I appreciate your efforts if you are trying to talk with me. But now I am thinking that this flashlight is just having some sort of malfunction. I am going to walk across the room now and pick it up and turn it all the way off.

Don't let me frighten you away." Then I walked over, picked up the flashlight, and turned the twist top a few times to see if it was loose or somehow malfunctioning. I determined that the flashlight appeared to be in normal, working condition, and I turned the light all the way off and set the flashlight back down on the floor.

By that time, it was probably about 8:00 p.m., and one of Savannah's notorious tour trolleys creeped by the house. I made the offhand remark that if the people on the trolley looked up into the attic window, they might see me and think I was a ghost! Well, the flashlight turned right on—and turned on very bright, I might add—when I made that comment! Bob experienced every hair on his body stand on end. We knew someone was with us.

When I began a series of questions related to anyone else being in the room with us besides the person that was trying to communicate with us, I saw a light turn all the way on, giving off a very bright and strong light. I watched the flashlight turn itself off. I then asked if there was someone there with us in the room that was trying to prevent the person we were communicating with from speaking with us further.

I watched the flashlight turn on and off, but just barely, so the result was a sort of flickering, low-energy level light. I stood silent and watched for a few seconds, and then it was over. The light turned itself all the way off. I recognized my own feelings of being drained. Although I knew the answer, I asked the question anyway. I said, "Are you still here with us? Let me know by turning one of those lights back on." We stayed another twenty minutes or so in the attic just in case someone decided to come back to us, but the session was over and there was nothing we could say to bring anyone back.

Whenever I see activity such as this with the flashlights, it always reminds me of how a child might behave. The sense that perhaps the person is having trouble using the light because they cannot figure out how it works, or perhaps they do not have enough energy to make it work properly. The other sense is that the person is actually just playing with the flashlights as if they are toys. The sporadic responses that we observed are in line with how a child might behave when they have a short attention span and aren't really listening to instructions from adults.

Lastly, I cannot discount the strong impression that I felt that someone entered the session we were having with the child spirit and essentially shut it down. Let me be clear that my impression was not "creepy" or otherwise ominous in any way. I simply had the impression that someone else was watching over the child we were attempting to communicate with and determined that the conversation should not go any further than it had already gone.

I will mention this, though. I took some interesting photos of those windows upstairs where we were doing our flashlight session. I know matrixing can make you believe that you are seeing faces in windows, but have a look for yourself at these consecutive shots and see what you make of these photos.

We were still sitting alone in the dark attic when we heard some commotion. A newlywed bride and her groom came rushing into the room, full wedding regalia and all. She gushed that they came to do a little ghost hunting. We left the happy couple to it.

When we returned to the Oglethorpe Room (304), we were greeted with luxurious bathrobes and a small assortment of fresh cookies. We stepped out onto our private balcony and gazed over our kingdom of Columbia Square. All was right in the world as far as we could tell. Nothing out of the ordinary happened to us in that room. I slept, as they say, like a rock. I would not let my mind think about the former funeral home days. If I got stuck on that train, I would not have been able to sleep until I returned home. I have explored and slept in some scary places in my life. But nothing scares me more than the thought of sleeping above the dead.

Look at the upper right corner of the window frame.
What do you see? This is a clean before shot.

Do you see a child's face in the right window, and another face in the middle? This photo was taken one second after the photo on the left.

What if they rose up and decided to start carrying on downstairs in the night? What if I ran into one on my way to get a snack? I don't think I could handle it. Luckily, the dead stayed asleep that night. If they were walking, they did not come for me that night.

Comments from Bob

As an outsider to the paranormal world, I always associated the word "haunted" with something evil, malicious, or scary. Learning through my travels with Jamie, I have come to realize that this is not always the case. Considered "The Most Haunted City in America," Savannah has a surprisingly positive vibe for the most part. Interestingly, the few areas that feel the most frightening are on the properties of some of the churches. As a resident of Savannah since 2010, I have loved the way Savannah feels. When it is cloudy, cold, and gray, it seems even more cozy and warm, if that is possible.

It was a rainy night in October when we arrived at the house. I almost expected a butler to answer the magnificent wooden door with a creepy Vincent Price-ish "Good Evening." I was surprised that what looked like a luxury home today was a workingman's home in the 1890s. I could imagine a happy home—children running up and down the stairs, playing, etc. I think that happy residual energy lingers today.

It felt haunted in the most heartwarming and nonthreatening way possible. There was a warm presence, a goodness, that was still there—a wholesome remnant spirit from early America. The attic had a welcoming "alive" and harmonious feel to it. I wondered how many men before me sat up there in that exact spot and looked over those streets contemplating the state of the nation.

From a ghost-hunting standpoint, I saw nothing that could not be explained logically until that moment when the flashlight sitting on the floor started lighting up in response to Jamie's questions. I had heard about Jamie's flashlight sessions, but I never knew what to think.

From an analytical and technical standpoint, the flashlights need something to complete the circuit to make the lights come on. It was evident that since these twist type flashlights did not move when they lit up, they were not being manually manipulated.

Instead, it was almost like the energy field of the alleged spirit was enough to complete the circuit without physically picking it up and twisting it to the on position. Could their energy be actively focused and manipulated to accomplish this? This is not without precedent, as many people report their camera and cell phone batteries mysteriously going dead in haunted places.

There are numerous accounts of spirits manipulating electronic devices and draining batteries. It is plausible that they can drain our emotional energy as well, as many people report feeling exhausted in haunted places.

Leaving the Kehoe House, I can say that my energy did not feel like it had been zapped, but I did feel a little foolish fully expecting Vincent Price and finding something warm and inviting, very much like the rest of Savannah feels.

If You Decide to Visit

Location & Contact Info

123 Habersham Street

Savannah, Georgia 31401

Tel: 1-800-820-1020 or 912-232-1020

E-mail: *innkeeper@kehoehouse.com*

Website: *www.kehoehouse.com*

Adults-only inn

Type of Tours & Hunts Offered

None directly. They recommend Oglethorpe Trolley Tours.

Size: 15,000 square feet (Renaissance Revival Mansion;
   13 guest rooms and an upstairs public loft space)

Price: weekly rates start at $180.00 per night (summer 2016)

Tips & Suggested Itinerary

If you only have a short weekend in Savannah, you can make the most of it by spending an afternoon wandering around. There are 22 squares that are public parks in the historic district. Forsyth Park is not to be missed, along with the jaw-dropping house gazing on Jones Street, Gaston Street, and Charlton Street. Get your coffee fix at the Sentient Bean when you arrive at Forsyth. Clary's Café is a Savannah institution for breakfast and lunch.

The Mercer House on Monterrey Square is the setting of the murder described in John Berendt's *Midnight in the Garden of Evil.* They give house tours daily.

There are a plethora of upscale shops and art galleries in the historic district, my favorites being One Fish Two Fish on Whitaker Street (home décor and accessories), and Kobo Gallery on Barnard Street. The Jepson Center is part of the Telfair Museums and contains contemporary art exhibits. Broughton Street has been newly redeveloped and is enjoying somewhat of a Renaissance period.

River Street is best viewed from above on the roof of the Bohemian Hotel at Rocks on the Roof.

Closest Airports

Savannah/Hilton Head International Airport (SAV)—
   about 20 minutes away from historic downtown Savannah

Hilton Head Airport (HHH)—about 39 miles away

Brunswick Golden Isles Airport (BQK)—about 73 miles away

Jacksonville International Airport (JAX)—about 130 miles away

FIVE

The 1886 Crescent Hotel
Eureka Springs, AR

As weird and strange as Jerome, Arizona, would later feel to me, Eureka Springs had the exact opposite feeling. I have never had a place, not to mention a whole town, resonate with me like the Crescent Hotel and Eureka Springs did. The place felt so good—like I didn't have one single care in the world anymore. Everything that I had been worrying about just didn't really seem to matter anymore. My life and purpose were completely in focus, and I had the deepest sense of peace that I was going to be okay. I was out of time, hidden away, and it was so comforting. I am not the only one to experience these feelings. In *Hidden History of Eureka Springs,* Joyce Zeller discusses the metaphysical energy that many first-time visitors report experiencing. Countless shopkeepers and innkeepers have heard a common phrase from visitors: "I don't know what it is about this place, but the minute I get here I begin to feel better. There's just something here."

The exterior of the 1886 Crescent Hotel.

The setting has got to have everything to do with this feeling. The fact that there are underground springs all over this Ozark Mountain town coupled with approximately fifty-four miles of limestone walls surely must contribute to all of the good energy I was picking up. Zeller wrote that many residents believe there are vortices around Grotto Spring as well as around the Crescent Hotel. Another theory in *Hidden History* suggests that all of the intense emotion from early visitors who came to the town seeking a cure could have left lingering energy. Zeller calls this "place memory," and I think I was picking up on this idea on my first visit to Eureka Springs.

History

My favorite short history that I consulted was Dr. D.R. Woolery's *The Grand Old Lady of the Ozarks*. Dr. Woolery explains that the Osage Indians are credited for first discovering the healing powers of the springs. Then, in 1854, Dr. Alvah Jackson brought his son to Basin Spring and bathed his eye that was injured while hunting in the water. Miraculously, the inflammation disappeared and Dr. Jackson began selling the miracle water in his office. After the Civil War, mountain health resorts were in vogue, and Eureka Springs became a boomtown of fifteen thousand people in the 1880s. The water, by the way, was claimed to cure about twenty-five ailments, and cancer was one of them.

Governor Powell Clayton was a member of the Eureka Springs Improvement Company and is credited for building the Crescent Hotel between 1884 and 1886. He also brought the Eureka Springs railroad to town. When the hotel first opened on May 1, 1886, it was called the "showplace of northwestern Arkansas." Paranormal investigators should take note that the hotel contains eighteen-inch-thick limestone walls. When the healing water fad ended, the hotel had to close for part of the season. By 1908 the Crescent College and Conservatory for Young Women was founded to operate in the hotel from September through May, with the hotel picking up operations for the summer months. This arrangement lasted through 1930 before opening again as a junior college. The junior college closed in 1933. Much of the furniture was sold to hotel guests from 1933 to 1937. Norman Baker bought the hotel in July 1937, and this is where things go a little dark. Since Baker's role in the building was so important in its history, and because his spirit is one of the most commonly reported apparitions, I felt that it was important to provide you with a brief history of who he was in life to better help you understand how his strong energy could still be contributing to modern-day hauntings at the hotel.

Norman Baker

Baker made his first $1.5 million fortune from his invention of the Tangley Air Calliope. In 1929, despite having no medical training whatsoever, he decided to open the Baker Hospital in his hometown of Muscatine, Iowa. He eventually got into trouble for practicing without a license and he abandoned ship. (Interestingly, one of the men he had partnered with, Harry Hoxsey, went on to become famous for his alleged cancer cure, the Hoxsey Herbal Treatment, which he used at a clinic in Dallas from 1930 through 1960, when the FDA was finally successful in banning the treatment in the United States. Hoxsey died of prostate cancer).

In *Border Radio, Quacks, Yodelers, Pitchmen, Psychics, and Other Amazing Broadcasters of the American Airwaves*, it is revealed that there was an investigation that discovered that the "Baker medicine" used to cure cancer was only "a mixture of carbolic acid, glycerin, alcohol, and a trace of peppermint oil." Another medicine Baker used in an attempt to cure cancer was watermelon seeds and corn silk that was boiled in water. Baker found his way to Eureka Springs along with his "Secret Remedy No. 5," and with full support and backing of many businesses in town, he moved his patients, staff, and alleged diploma-mill physicians to Arkansas and opened his second Baker Hospital inside the Crescent Hotel. (The town paper, *The Daily Times-Echo*, essentially gave the opinion that if Baker did well, then the town would do well.) In his autobiography, Baker wrote about always having a gun within reach, adding how his office in Muscatine was an armed fortress. Given what we know of his paranoia, it is completely believable that he would carry on in the same manner in Eureka Springs. Dr. Woolery also wrote that Baker kept two submachine guns hanging on the wall of his private quarters (what is now known as the Governor's Suite). We were told on a tour that he kept armed guards in the parking lot.

The man had awful taste and painted the inside of the building with shades of purple, red, orange, black, and yellow. He drove around in a ridiculous lavender car and was fond of outfitting himself in the same color.

To understand the full extent of the craziness of this common shyster, you really have to read the autobiography he commissioned in 1936.

Doctors, Dynamiters, and Gunmen details the full extent of paranoid delusions and illusions of grandeur suffered by Baker. He claimed that the hospital in Muscatine is "one of the world's most important health centers." He claimed that AMA stands for "Amateur Meatcutters' Association," and M.D. means "more dough." He was convinced that the AMA sent three men to his office who were trying to kill him, and he kept himself armed at all times. His own definition of a quack was painted over the reception door in Muscatine. It read: "A quack is one who thinks and does things others can't do."

He finally got himself convicted of mail fraud in 1940 because of the pamphlets he was mailing out. (One example of his direct mailings was "Where Sick Folks Get Well.") More trouble from Iowa also caught up to him. Back in 1929, he took five test patients and gave them his cancer cure. Every single one was dead within the year, yet Baker published a magazine article stating that all of his test patients had improved after taking his cure. Major selling points advertised for the Baker Hospital included claims that "We do not remove any organs in the treatment of any ailment. No operations, radium, or X-ray used." He only served four years in Leavenworth (March 1941–July 1944), and his mug shot is in the public domain all over the Internet, but it was also produced by the National Archives Record Center.

In Stephen Spence's "Pure Hoax" article, he writes that the psychiatrist in Leavenworth determined that Baker suffered from delusions and honestly believed that he had done nothing wrong. Spence follows that up with Baker's last-known words on the subject: "If I could keep my radio station open, I would make a million dollars out of the suckers of the states." The chance at seeing Baker's prison file was too tempting to pass up, so I paid my hundred dollars and bought myself a ticket to his show. When the file came, I had an entertaining evening of reading all of the historic psychiatric evaluations that were completed during his imprisonment.

The following traits about Baker were noted:

- He has a superior manipulative ability.

- He was a person of very overbearing disposition. He appears to believe that the American Medical Association and the Aluminum Trust have been and are persecuting him. It is our belief that he may be a mental case.

- He appears to be a high-class promoter and swindler. His speech was noticeably affected in an effort to make a heavy impression on the listener. Insofar as his future is concerned he will probably be a faker and swindler always.

- He has been an advertising quack who, in capitalizing on the gullibility of cancer victims, has with other individuals, largely under his domination, succeeded in making a great deal of money.

- This man is possessed of considerable intelligence and ability, and could have, and still may be able to, devote these talents to good use. For many years, however, he has devoted them entirely to illegal, vicious, and cruel practices in leading cancer victims to spend money for worthless treatment.

Baker lived out the rest of his life on a yacht and died in 1958 from cancer, just like his former business partner.

The Crescent Hotel reopened in 1946 and had a series of owners until 1997, when Marty and Elise Roenigk purchased the hotel and restored it to its original grand condition. The couple also purchased and renovated downtown's Basin Park Hotel. Tragically, Marty died in a car crash in 2009.

Lori Menichetti discusses his experience as part of the remodeling crew of the Crescent. He wrote, "I found many of the bedroom closets had trap-doors, with stairways into hidden passages." One of the biggest rumors that we heard concerning what was found during renovations was that human skeletons were found within the walls. I have not found any reputable written report or oral histories to support that claim, although it is certainly plausible given the building's history.

Visiting The Crescent

It was complete happenstance that Bob and I even wound up at the Crescent when we did. Bob is a pilot, and I was tagging along with him on a business trip to Oklahoma. The Crescent is a clear front-runner for the title of "America's Most Haunted Hotel," and it had been on my radar for many years. I had just never managed to make it out for a visit. A few hours before we were scheduled to return back to Atlanta, I asked Bob if Eureka Springs would by chance be on our way home. It turned out that it was indeed on our way home, the Crescent had a vacancy, and so it was settled.

To me, the intrigue of the hotel lies in all of the mysterious tales told about the days when Norman Baker turned the old Crescent College and Conservatory for Young Women into a cancer hospital in 1937. Norman Baker is a convicted criminal and quack who made about four million dollars doing things such as injecting carbolic acid right into tumors and giving his patients spring water to drink to cure cancer. Today, Norman Baker's former cancer hospital is a proud member of the Historic Hotels of America, and it is a fully renovated destination hotel on top of a hill in Eureka Springs, Arkansas. The hotel interior is red and black, and while it seems very macabre, I did not feel that effect at all. I found the place to be very peaceful and welcoming, yet it also felt highly charged. The building itself felt alive. Quite bluntly, the place felt haunted as hell. Despite all of the tragic tales from the hospital days, I did not feel any sadness here. There is even a chimney outside the Sky Bar that is still painted purple from Norman Baker's eccentric time.

We arrived in the midst of prime wedding season and actually saw two different wedding parties that day. The hotel is breathtaking and full of ornate details, such as this owl carving in the fireplace.

The owl carving in the fireplace at the Crescent.

Norman Baker's desk is located in the lobby of the hotel.

The hexagonal desk that Norman Baker used from 1937 to 1939 sits in a corner of the lobby after being moved from what is now the Governors Suite room of the hotel. He used a different drawer for each one of his business ventures.

Stephanie Stodden, director of operations at the Eureka Springs Historical Museum, was kind enough to share her research from her archives. These historical photos of the Baker Hospital are absolute gems! We can appreciate the lobby, common areas, and hallway views, and we can see what a typical patient bedroom would have looked like. There's even a glimpse of what appears to be Norman Baker at work.

Despite the crowds in the midst of summer, the back porches were absolute havens of respite. It must have been a well-kept secret that guests could access all levels of the porches, because we had uninterrupted access to all of them.

We enjoyed them immensely, although I have read much criticism about the concrete porches because Norman Baker destroyed the original wooden balconies and replaced them with concrete.

A photo of the lobby when the Baker Hospital was in operation.

Norman Baker is pictured at his desk.

The back porch of the Crescent.

While swimming in the pool, I looked up and suddenly knew that the building I was looking at used to house the servants (a fact that was confirmed on the ghost tour later that evening).

While resting in our bedroom before dinner (around 4:40 p.m. or so), I looked at the seafoam-colored walls and blurted out, "This is when I die."

Later, while wandering alone around the west wing of the hotel, I was drawn to walk down a staircase and was overcome by a smell that can only be described as strange and old.

I inhaled as deeply as I could, but I could not place the smell. When I returned after the ghost tour, the smell was gone. This is the singular experience of my lifetime where I have felt such strange things about a place that seemed to come to me intuitively. I was having vivid impressions.

The ghost tour will tell you all the popular legends and stories and will even lead you through the modern day spa, past the laundry room, and straight into the former morgue, where the original autopsy table used by Norman Baker still sits.

Ghost Tour

There are tales told of Norman Baker building secret passages going under the hotel into town, burning bodies in the incinerator, and sending pre-written patient letters out to family members after a patient died to continue receiving money for the deceased patient's treatment. He was supposed to have erected steel shutters on the third floor to separate the terminal patients who were succumbing to disease and making too much noise. When it was all over, they say he wheeled them down to the morgue in the wee hours of the night to perform his autopsies.

The hotel is made of limestone, and this is thought to contribute to some of the hauntings. Some people believe that certain staircases within the hotel are vortexes. It is unknown how many patients died in Baker's Hospital.

An original wheelchair from the Baker Hospital.

When we went on the ghost tour, I was taken aback by how many tales of full-body apparitions were recounted. The cast of characters is quite large. They include:

The Nurse

There is allegedly an apparition of a nurse pushing a gurney down the hallways at night. She has never been reported to communicate with anyone, but witnesses have claimed that the wheels of the gurney emit a squeaking noise. This only happens at night, as though it is a residual imprint from when Baker used to order the dead bodies be transported down to the morgue while the living patients slept.

Ghosts in the Crystal Dining Room

Reports range from a single man who sits in silence at the bar, but mysteriously disappears, to a full-fledged party of ghosts wearing Victorian clothing that appear to be attending a dinner party.

Victorian Gentleman

Reports frequently cite the lobby and bar area of the hotel. Many believe that this apparition who is formally dressed, complete with a top hat, is none other than former hotel physician, Dr. Ellis, whose office was kept in room 212.

Theodora

Theodora is thought to be an elderly cancer patient who still walks the halls of the hotel. Theodora is reported to interact with people. She can be seen fumbling with her keys outside of room 419. She has also been blamed for packing the bags of hotel guests who dare criticize their accommodations.

Small Boy

Our tour guide also told us that around 3:00 a.m. a residual image of a four-year-old boy, referred to as "Brecky," can be seen around room 226 bouncing a ball and angrily saying, "It's just not fair." It is thought that he was the son of the owner of the girls' school and died of appendicitis at the age of four.

Former College Student

There have also been reports of a female apparition that has been sighted walking in the garden. The story is that she either committed suicide or fell from the fourth floor balcony. Witnesses have also told hotel employees that they have seen a misty apparition fall from this balcony.

Michael

Room 218 is the home of the Michael sightings. Michael is said to have been a seventeen-year-old Irish stonemason who fell to his death while working in the hallway right outside this room. He is said to be very mischievous and will hide items and adjust the thermostat in the room. Some guests have reportedly claimed that they have seen his arms coming out of the bathroom mirror, that they have woken up in the morning to find that the walls appear to be covered in blood, and even that they have woken up to find themselves sleeping in a pool of blood.

In 2005 a full-body apparition was caught with a thermal imaging camera in the morgue by Syfy's *Ghost Hunters*. The apparition appears to be wearing a stonemason's cap. Could this have been Michael?

Norman Baker

Witnesses have claimed to see a lost-looking Baker pacing back and forth around the former recreation room. Apparently he is still fond of wearing his signature white suit with a purple or lavender shirt to complete his outfit.

I maintained a healthy skepticism while on the tour and especially while standing first in the dark morgue and then inside the former walk-in cooler where Baker used to store cadavers and assorted body parts. Because we were with a group, it was impossible to conduct any sort of EVP session, and nothing registered on the guide's K-II meter. Still, I certainly believe that many of the reported stories are possibly true. It is extremely difficult for me to get in tune with a building's atmosphere when I am standing in line or in a crowd. It just doesn't feel like anything to me, but it was a fun and educational tour that took us into an off-limits area of the hotel.

After dinner we set off walking the grounds of Crescent Park. We wound up on a heavily wooded and shaded trail into town. The entire town is a nationally protected historic district, and as we kept walking, the town itself even had an effect on me. I was convinced that I had walked these paths before. Maybe it was all the hidden, swirling, underground healing waters creating some type of energy vortex.

I wanted to see if I could locate any possible underground tunnel entrances around the hills near the hotel. Over on the *Underground Eureka* website, the last report written states that the secret tunnels rumored to be underneath the hotel remain elusive, despite many surveying efforts ("The Crescent Connection"). Downtown Eureka Springs does offer walking tours into some underground areas of the city.

As we steadily climbed back up the hill to the hotel, Bob and I heard a haunting melody being played. There was a strange little boy sitting out on the front porch of a cottage playing a xylophone. He was all by himself—with no other soul in sight. As I passed his line of vision, he looked at me with unblinking eyes, like those of an old, world-weary woman. While staring at me, he didn't miss a beat on the xylophone.

I kept walking, covered in goose bumps, despite the ninety-degree heat.

A few months after our stay, I was reading Margaret Wayt Debolt's *Savannah Spectres* where she writes, "The Irish once believed that on

St. John's Eve, June 23, souls visited the place where they would meet death." I was covered in chills as I read that passage, as this was the date of my first stay. While I do not have any traditional paranormal-type experiences to report from my visit, I am unable to deny the strong feelings of déjà vu I experienced while in the building, walking the grounds, and walking through the entire town. This was the first time in my life that I seriously started to consider and wonder about the feasibility of past lives. I also began to wonder about other beings masquerading as humans in the light of day. The boy was odd.

The Morning After: Breakfast in the Crystal Dining Room

Over breakfast the next morning, for the first time in all of my travels, I was dreading going home and being separated from Bob. It felt as though I was getting heartsick. We had learned the day before of the Crescent Hotel's history as a girls' college in the early 1900s, and had discussed the possibility of a past life explaining my feelings toward the hotel and the town itself. Bob reflected that he had experienced similar type feelings at an airport in Texas. We wondered if we had spent a previous moment in time, sitting on the same back porch, talking with each other one summer night long ago.

Sitting in the dining room that morning, I had an overwhelming sensation that I was wasting my life, and I didn't want to do it anymore. To make a long story shorter, my experience in Eureka Springs that morning in the Crystal Dining Room, was the catalyst for me leaving Atlanta and starting a new life in Savannah with Bob. Within two months of returning home from that trip, we had successfully moved me to Savannah. We didn't want to wait any longer to start our life together.

Comments from Bob

As I mentioned being a neophyte to official paranormal phenomena, I am in more of a "receive and observe" mode rather than a "transmit from the position-of-authority mode." There have been enough personal experiences in my life to give credence to the theory that there is something there, even though we cannot pick it up, weigh it, measure it, and develop scientific theories.

There have been things I have seen and felt that cannot be explained logically, or if they can, the logical explanation is as questionable as some of the paranormal explanations, which brings us to Eureka Springs. I have found that there are some towns and cities that have their own presence, as I mentioned in some of the other chapters. Contrary to the unnerving uneasiness felt in Bisbee and Jerome, Eureka Springs had a welcoming feel.

Situated in a beautiful mountain setting, the Crescent Hotel had a feel that I have come to recognize as a haunted feel. This one, however, was not threatening or spooky, but rather warm and welcoming, yet still harboring a haunted uneasiness that can be sensed.

On the ghost tour Jamie mentioned, I was touched by some of the stories. I did not sense or experience anything I would consider relatable to the stories we heard, but while I make a concerted effort to disregard my imagination in these settings, as the imaginary can easily be confused with actual, it was easy for the mind's eye to imagine what the stories told.

Hearing about Norman Baker running around secret passageways carrying a tommy gun was very believable. I imagine it took a great deal of energy to stay one step ahead of the law. Hearing the stories about how much hope he gave to cancer patients was a tragic reminder of the willingness of some to exploit the weaknesses, sicknesses, and fears of very gullible and fragile people who will believe anything and pay everything if it means they will feel better. It's tragic to hear he failed to deliver on the promise and how they concealed the patient deaths while the bodies stacked to the ceiling in the morgue.

The apparition of a little boy bouncing the ball saying, "it's not fair," is very plausible to me. Here was a young boy full of hope and vigor and wonder, a life of bouncing balls and playgrounds and trees to climb and awesome things. Imagine this life just getting started and having it suddenly taken away because of a tummy ache. It is very easy to imagine that young spirit, robbed of life and separated from his body, being confused and very upset that his life was taken away. I believe this was residual energy imprinted by a very strong emotional reaction to a very unfair event. Regardless, I hope this young spirit has found peace in the life beyond.

The most vivid experience I had here, other than noticing the warm and welcoming ambiance, was seeing Jamie's very powerful reaction to it. I have never seen Jamie have such a connection to a place, and that has led us into some very interesting conversations about past lives, something that we may explore together down the road.

If You Decide to Visit

Location & Contact Info

75 Prospect Avenue

Eureka Springs, Arkansas 72632

Tel: (855) 725-5720

E-mail: *concierge.crescent@gmail.com*

Website: *www.crescent-hotel.com/*
www.americasmosthauntedhotel.com

Type of Tours & Hunts Offered

Nightly ghost tours at 8:00 p.m. Adults $22.50; children 12 & under $8.00

Size: 72 rooms, 4 floors.

Price: weekly rates start at $169.86 (summer 2016). Always check their website for discounts for Sunday–Thursday night stays. Some nights can be booked for as low as $129.00!

Tips & Suggested Itinerary

Enjoy the atmosphere of the hotel and downtown Eureka, which is very, very cool. Take a walk from the hotel parking lot and check out all the natural springs on your way to shop and dine downtown. The guide I used can be found here: *http://www.eurekaspringsonline.com/2014/10 /eureka-springs-natural-springs-trail-2/*. Have a few vacation days left over? Burn rubber out of town and explore the Arkansas Art Trail.

Closest Airports

Northwest Arkansas Regional Airport (XNA)—about 49 miles away

Branson Airport (BKG)—about 54 miles away

Springfield-Branson National Airport (SGF)—about 95 miles away

SIX

The Jerome Grand Hotel
Jerome, AZ

To roll into town as an outsider and write about Jerome feels fraudulent. I have only been there twice, but each time the car crept up mile-high Cleopatra Hill, I knew I was seeing something special (and quite possibly entering *The Twilight Zone*). If you are coming in as a day-tripper, you might stick your head out the window and admire the rows of galleries, retail shops, and restaurants. But if you are paying attention and stop to enjoy a quiet moment alone, you might notice a certain eeriness in the air. You might start to suspect that there is something going on underneath the surface of this town that goes a little bit deeper than the ghost town tourism industry. You would be right.

History

Jerome was a copper mining community with two mines—the United Verde Copper Company and the United Verde Extension (UVX, or "Little Daisy").

The exterior of the Jerome Grand Hotel.

The town once had a thriving population of fifteen thousand. William A. Clark, a senator from Montana, purchased the United Verde Copper Company in 1888 from H.J. Allen and built several railroad lines, including the San Pedro, Salt Lake, and Los Angeles Lines. James Douglas, Jr. owned the UVX and built a mansion in town that is currently a state park. Jerome was nicknamed "The Billion Dollar Copper Camp."

After Clark and his son died in the mid-1930s, the Phelps Dodge Corporation won control of the United Verde Copper Company. By 1953 Phelps Dodge closed the mine, and according to Diane Rapaport, author of *Home Sweet Jerome,* the population dwindled to 132 adults and 87 children. When the mines closed, what remained was 88 miles of tunnels. Or, as Rapaport so distinctly puts it, "When Jerome's underground city became a lifeless catacomb that contained what was once the town's lifeblood." Hollywood would have us believe that mining is a romantic and prosperous industry. That is certainly true for the executives. But the miners would most likely tell a very different tale. In fact, Roberto Rabago, a retired attorney who grew up in Jerome as the son of a miner, paints a very different picture of life in a mining town in his 2011 book entitled *Rich Town Poor Town: Ghosts of Copper's Past*. Although it is billed as fiction, he does state that the core elements of the stories are true. He compares Jerome to an ancient slave labor camp. There is one particular quote from his "Father's Day" story that gives me chills every time I read it: "You go into a black world that will kill you with a misstep. It's a world that some miners believe is even beyond the realm of God."

Bear in mind part of Jerome's history is blatantly discussed in Herbert V. Young's *They Came to Jerome* (which was published in 1972, long after his retirement). Young worked as secretary to the general manager of the United Verde Copper Company from 1912 to 1955. Oftentimes, Young's writing almost reads as homage to the wealthy town residents. It is clear from his writing that he admires and possibly is in awe of all of the powerful men who employed him. But even Young is unable to deny the influence and power held by the executives, realizing how that power and influence controlled the news outlets in Jerome. Case in point: a smallpox epidemic struck the town in 1901–1902, yet *The Jerome Mining News* did not publish any details and refused to disclose the number of deaths. Further, he claims that 1907 was the worst year for mine deaths, with thirteen men perishing in the United Verde Mine. H.J. Allen allegedly asserted his power and influence to kill Jerome's first newspaper. *The Jerome Chronicle* operated for just a few months in 1895. Its owner Herbert Eugene Wilcox reportedly met with Allen in an attempt to write about the mines. Allen denied him access, and when he attempted to do a little bit of investigative journalism, he angered Allen. Young does not tell us exactly how the paper died, just that Wilcox ran a notice in his own paper on June 1, 1895, that announced the paper had ceased operation. In contrast to Wilcox, William S. Adams started *The Arizona Mining News* in 1895, which was in publication for about forty years. In describing why Adams was more successful and allowed to operate, Young explains that "Adams knew how to get along. He allied himself with the copper company. He never crossed that corporation in any way and was ever ready to praise it and its owners and management and to support its political favorites. In return he received financial support." Allen's control of the news continued with the succession of William Clark. Young explains that the news outlets were tightly controlled by the Company: "As fame of the United Verde expanded many journalists visited Jerome and wrote stories about it. They found little cooperation from the mine officials, for Senator Clark would permit but a minimum of information to be given out, especially of the underground mine." In 1918 a paper called *The Jerome Sun* came to an abrupt end because the company seized its printing press. I outline these events to demonstrate how the power of the company officials would undoubtedly trickle into the operations of the United Verde Hospital, and even into the lives of the entire town's population. The company was in control.

The short version of how Jerome grew from an abandoned ghost town to a tourist destination is that the members of the Jerome Historical Society got together and created the concept of a "Ghost City" to entice tourists to come and patronize their new Mine Museum. Hippies and artists flocked to the city for rock bottom home prices and freedom. There was a drug bust in 1985 that made the *New York Times*, and the town today, with a population that is still under five hundred, sees a thriving tourism industry. Some have said they enjoy *too* many tourists. Living in Savannah, I know just what they mean.

The Land Itself, Disease, Deportation, and Deaths

Before the mining companies came to town and set up shop, the land was home to the Yavapai Indians. Mark C. Frederick authored a research paper ("Cough, Gasp, Wheeze" The Role of Disease in Jerome's Past") in 2000 for *The Jerome Chronicle*, which was a quarterly newsletter for the Jerome Historical Society. He estimates that their population may have dwindled from 3,000 down to 2,000–2,500 during a smallpox epidemic before the 1860s. Frederick reports how a U.S. Army surgeon said, "'Deaths were so frequent that the bodies were left in their oowas which were burned over them or they were left to mummify in the dry air, as there were not enough well Indians to cut and carry the wood with which to burn the dead, as was their custom.'"

In the late 1800s, Jerome had a series of four major fires. The town had epidemics of typhoid fever in 1891 and another smallpox epidemic in 1899 that was large enough to require a pest house be built to contain sufferers. The scarlet fever epidemic came in 1907, and the 1918 Spanish influenza was reported to have caused 131 deaths in October and November. Ann Hopkins is quoted saying that "'the miners were dropping like rats, due to the high altitude, and the condition of their lungs working in the mines'" (Frederick). The year 1924 brought another smallpox epidemic. The article also reveals that what we call Silicosis today was at the time referred to as miner's lung or Consumption. The results can cause pneumonia and heart failure, and the miners were more likely to develop lung cancer and tuberculosis. The historical society's funeral records from the 1940s showed that a third of all deaths for the town were medically unexplained. Within that category would be accidents, suicides, and murders.

In May of 1917, workers entered into a strike that ultimately ended on July 10, 1917, with a citizens' posse of two hundred men that rounded up an estimated one hundred workers and loaded them like animals onto cattle cars, which were provided by the United Verde Copper Company. The train hauled the men out of town and left them in Kingman, Arizona, with the order to never return. This event is thought to have been a practice run for what would occur just two days later in Bisbee. There were no consequences to the mining companies for the mass kidnappings.

During the late 1920s and early 1930s, many downtown buildings were lost because of landslides. You cannot help but wonder if all of this instability has an effect today. What impact might living in a town that is built over eighty-eight miles of catacombs, where an unknown amount of miners undoubtedly met their traumatic deaths, have on a person's psyche? There have been a number of modern suicide reports in the town where men have walked up the hill in the vicinity of the old hospital and committed suicide. Nobody seems to know why.

Contributing to the sadness and tragedy of the town is the story of Father John, which can be found in Rapaport's book. The gist of it is that the poor man was found in his room within the Holy Family Catholic Church. It is unknown whether he had suffered a stroke or some other medical condition, but he had to be carted out of there on a stretcher, reportedly shouting "Hospitale no!" Admittedly, older people (and men in particular) can be found to be adverse to receiving medical treatment. But given everything I have read about the weirdness of Jerome, it is enough to make me wonder if there was any specific reason that Father John did not want to go to the hospital on the hill.

The United Verde Hospital

Quality of Care

In 1983, Dr. Walter V. Edwards wrote an article entitled "Jerome Takes Its Medicine II." Edwards writes that Phelps Dodge had one chief surgeon employed in Jerome in 1946, stating that "the Company Hospital in Jerome was active and well operated" and "Phelps Dodge Employees and their families were provided almost complete prepaid medical and hospital care." He goes on to report that John McMillan, a retired miner and mortician, held the opinion that the employees really had a good thing going for them with the hospital. However, isn't life always grand when painted by the surviving executives and those who lived arguably privileged lives?

In the above-mentioned article, a different picture is reported by the son of Patrick Riordan. His father was a foreman who came down with silicosis and was taken care of by the company. The son went on to write, "Not many of the miners who came to Jerome were so honored." *Rich Town Poor Town* contains many stories that do not reflect highly on the quality of care inside the hospital. Even with the knowledge that this is fiction, it plants a seed of what might happen in a company-owned private hospital when the needs of the patient directly conflict with the bottom-line numbers of the company. What happened to the patients who had been injured beyond hope for returning to the mines? Did they continue to receive lifelong health care, or were they transferred to the death room or discharged and let go from their jobs? If the latter transpired, maybe this explains much of the negative feelings that many have reported inside the building today.

Dr. Arthur C. Carlson was the chief surgeon from 1921 until 1945. In Dr. Edwards's paper, he talks about a high turnover rate for physicians and quotes Dr. Hilton as telling him, "As you probably know, A.C. Carlson wasn't the easiest person to get along with."

However, Dr. Carlson was also written up as "one of the most capable and successful young physicians in his section of the state." Whatever type of physician he might have been, it appears to me that he was a company man. What happens when his duty as a physician to his patients conflicts with his duty as an employed physician for the company?

I don't know, but reading between the lines of all of these articles coupled with the darkness that many have felt inside this building makes me pose the question. Maybe it is a question without merit and based on speculation. Still, I wonder. It comes from my background as a civil litigation trial paralegal that has seen both sides of medical malpractice lawsuits.

The world is a hard place, and with or without Dr. Carlson playing any kind of role in the matter, the cold hard truth is that patients die inside hospitals. They die when the money runs out, just as they die in spite of receiving the best medical care that money can buy, completely absent of any negligence or malpractice issues whatsoever.

I'm wondering how quickly the money ran out for the care of someone who was never going to be able to make money for the company again, and what sort of impact that might have left behind. I would not expect to hear that great amounts of time, energy, and funds were allocated to the long-term care and well-being of an amputated miner and his family. It sounds like a recipe for some lingering bad mojo if you ask me.

What's more, the Jerome Historical Society has limited documents about the hospital. Many records were destroyed and thrown down mine shafts when the hospital closed. Much of what was left was destroyed by weather or vandalized when the building went vacant.

Visiting the Jerome Grand Hotel

The Jerome Grand Hotel was purchased in 1994 by the Altherr family from Phelps Dodge. The hotel was originally the fourth hospital in Jerome. It was in operation from January 1927 until 1950 when the mine began to slow down. I have read that even though it was closed, it was maintained until the early 1970s in case of an emergency.

The Altherr family has worked to preserve the building, and walking through, especially in a slow period where you might not see many other guests, it feels like stepping back in time. Just down the hill the third hospital still stands, affectionately called "the clubhouse," but it is not open to the public. The owners very much embrace the hotel's haunted history, and tours and ghost hunts are held weekly.

Some of the original features that still exist inside the Jerome Grand Hotel include the 1926 Otis Elevator, which, according to the hotel's website, is claimed to be the "oldest original self-service elevator in Arizona and possibly the United States."

It is a slow, somewhat creepy ride to the top of the building, and I dare you to take a ride and *not* think about what happened to Claude Harvey while you are waiting for your floor.

We scheduled a ghost tour and hunt package for the night of our stay, but when we arrived, we were told it was cancelled because we were the only ones booked into the hotel for the evening! I could not believe my good fortune, and it was getting even better when hotel employee Tom Lennox told us he could accommodate us on a private tour.

The hotel shared some helpful resource tools with us, including a list of people who died in the building and a map outlining what they believe all the former rooms to be. The conservative estimate of deaths inside the building is placed at around nine hundred.

Reflecting upon what you have now read about the miners, silicosis, and tuberculosis, does it come as any surprise to you that one of the most highly reported phenomena experienced by guests inside the Jerome Grand Hotel are the phantom sounds of coughing and labored breathing?

The first stop was to go to the boiler room from the lobby (the old ER entrance). We were then shown the death sites of Claude Harvey and Manoah Hoffpauir ("Hoff").

Mr. Harvey was found facedown underneath the elevator in 1935. His death was ruled an accident, but there is much speculation as to the truth of this.

Tom said that many people in town were waiting for him to retire so they could put in to take over his job.

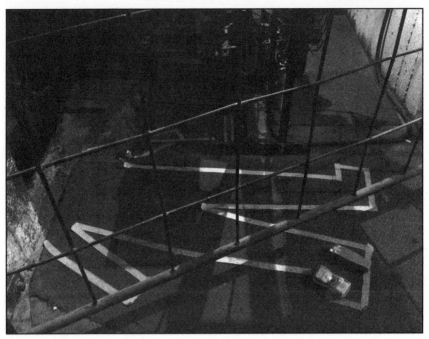

The location where Harvey's body was found is marked on the floor.

If he was working the night shift in a hospital and witnessed something that someone wanted to erase, staging an "accident" was a good way to get rid of him. I was very intrigued by the legend of Claude Harvey and was able to conduct some independent research while I was in town.

The Death of Claude Harvey

According to Claude McLeod Harvey's death certificate, he was born on February 20, 1872, in Aberdeen, Scotland. He died on April 3, 1935, at 6:45 a.m. and was buried two days later.

The manner of injury was listed as a descending elevator, and the cause of death was determined to be "crushed head, result of an accident, according to verdict of coroner's jury."

The location where Hoffpauir was found is marked in the boiler room.

Colleen Holt of the Jerome Historical Society found a copy of the coroner's inquest in their archives. The inquest appears to have been held less than six hours after Mr. Harvey was found. The members sworn to act as the coroner's jury were J.G. Crowley, J.P. Connolly, H.W. Eldridge, E.E. McFarland, J.S. Prosser, and Henry Weigand.

The first two witnesses were sworn to testify:

- Gladys Morton: Nurse on duty who first noticed something was wrong with the elevator; she called John Zivkovich to the scene.

- John Zivkovich: Hospital engineering and maintenance worker called to the scene by Ms. Morton; took Mr. Harvey's position after his death.

Zivkovich said that he and Harvey were in Harvey's bedroom talking at about 6:40 a.m. Zivkovich left to get his overalls, and three minutes after that, Gladys Morton called him to say the elevator was making a noise. He went to the basement and found Harvey lying under the elevator.

Q: What was the position of the body?

A: His head was under the elevator with his shoulders sticking out, his body was hunched up and he was lying on his face and the elevator was on his neck. When I saw that I went and told the girl and she called Mr. Henson, and he was lying in the same position when he saw him.

His opinion was that it must have been an accident because the elevator moves slowly, and Harvey would have seen it coming down on him.

T.C. Henson was the electrician foreman for Upper Verde Public Utilities; Ms. Morton called him at home around 6:45 a.m. to come to the scene. Upon arrival, the motor was still running in the elevator so he cut the current and threw the switch. Henson testified:

Q: What position was he in when you saw him first?

A: His body was on the stomach with head out of sight as if he might have been looking down the sump, was my first opinion.

Q: Have you any theory of your own as to how it was brought about?

A: I couldn't say, but my first impression was that it was possible that I might [sic] have been looking down the shaft to find the trouble. Later on it was apparent that there was a cut on top of the head, and I thot [sic] he might have been standing up listening, as I have done myself. When Dr. Carlson washed off the blood there was only a small wound just behind the right ear a little to the center.

He had no suspicion of foul play. Apparently someone pushed the button and called the elevator to the basement.

Q: Could the elevator have been worked from where the deceased was found?

A: I could work it from down there, but none of the men up there know how, it is a case of knowing how to move it in an emergency, I use two sticks to manipulate the switch.

Q: Are you positive he did not know how to start it?

A: Yes, I am positive.

Q: Could Mr. Harvey have called the elevator to the basement and have walked down there by the time the elevator got there?

A: Yes, there would be lots of time, if on an upper floor, to be there before it got there.

Dr. Menno S. Gaede: Someone named Mrs. Lyle called Dr. Menno S. Gaede to the scene around 6:50 a.m. His testimony read:

I was called by phone by Mrs. Lyle at ten minutes to seven and got there five minutes later … and was immediately taken back into the engine room where Mr. Harvey was found head pinned under the elevator, prone position, legs extended, left arm under chest, right hand close to face. He did not show any signs of life. I removed the left arm to get stethoscope close to heart, found no heart beats and no breath sounds in lungs. After I had examined Mr. Harvey, the cage was moved and I pulled Mr. Harvey back about eighteen inches to further examine him, grabbing his belt with my right hand, under the head I put my left hand. Found a streak of blood in the middle of the forehead from scratch, there was a cut back of the right ear, blood coming from nose and had also run into mouth. The right hand was paler in color than the left hand, apparently due to pressure. That is about all I observed.

Q: Other witnesses have previously testified the man was killed by having been struck by descending cage, is this your belief?

A: Yes. Probably pressure on back of neck was immediate cause of death … It appears to be an accident, altho [sic] a very peculiar one.

It is unclear from the record who John S. Riordan is. Perhaps he was with the medical examiner's office because all he did was read out vital statistics of Mr. Harvey upon observation. He did not give direct testimony.

Dr. A.C. Carlson: Chief Surgeon

Dr. Carlson explains the position of the hospital: "Mr. Zivkovich says that he did not start the elevator and if it is possible that anyone else did and found that an accident had occurred would not go away. I believe that Mr. Harvey actually brought that elevator to that floor, regardless of how. For, as I say, there was no one there but Miss Morton, Mrs. Harrington, and the cook and dishwasher."

The transcript from the inquest is a little odd to me for several reasons. The first is that Dr. Carlson was not the doctor who examined the body at the scene. Why is he even there? He is there because he is the chief surgeon for the company and he has to assert his authority to do damage control. Judge Smith does not subject him to any questioning whatsoever. In fact, we do not know the circumstances of how Dr. Carlson even came to find out about Mr. Harvey's death. That is certainly a bit of detail that would seem relevant, yet he is never asked and he does not volunteer that piece of information. This leaves a lot of room for what is known within the legal field as "damage control." Who called Dr. Carlson and what did they tell him? Who did Dr. Carlson call within the company, and what did they direct him to do? All of these questions would certainly be discoverable, but we never get that far in this case.

There are a few employees who are mentioned throughout the transcript but are also mysteriously never questioned: the dishwasher on duty, the cook, Vivian Harrington, and someone who would later become the town's most famous nurse—Mattie Leyel. Why were none of these employees included with the inquest? Did Dr. Carlson assert his authority to keep them from being questioned? Also, there was no autopsy ordered, which is also incredibly suspicious. The final verdict was read. Let the record show: "Claude Harvey came to his death by being caught under the elevator at the United Verde Hospital. The accident being unavoidable, we exonerate the Company from all blame." It really makes you wonder. It seems so unusual to include such specific language in an attempt to "exonerate the Company." Because of the manner and speed in which this inquest was held, I am only left with two possible conclusions, none of which create a good legacy for the company. It would seem that either Mr. Harvey was outright murdered and the company exerted their power to control the inquest and avoid an independent autopsy being conducted, *or* Mr. Harvey did meet an unfortunate accident and the company exerted their power and control to make sure they avoided any responsibility for his death and effectively avoided litigation by ensuring that no independent autopsy was done.

I was able to obtain a CD of an oral history interview that Mattie Leyel gave in 1974. The original is on file at the Sharlot Hall Museum in Prescott, Arizona. The gist of it was that she loved her career as a nurse, Dr. Carlson was an excellent doctor and orthopedist, the hospital was wonderful, and everyone received excellent care. Honestly, did anyone think she was going to say otherwise?! One other thing that was of interest to me was that there were three patients, by the names of Boxcar Riley, Handsome Dan Murphy, and Elderberry Bill, who were permanent residents of the hospital. Mattie said they did not have anyone to take care of them, so they just stayed at the hospital until they died. For whatever reason, Mattie did not leave anything behind in her oral history that made any reference whatsoever to Claude Harvey. This almost makes me even more suspicious about his death.

Hoff

Hoff was a maintenance man who lived in the vacant hospital while taking care of the building for Phelps Dodge. According to the story, he had a drinking problem coupled with some family problems and, as a result, took his own life. When he failed to show up in town at his favorite bar, a cop came looking for him and started on the top floor of the building, leaving the building dark as he patrolled the area. He worked his way all the way down to the boiler room, through the hallway, and around a corner before he found Hoff standing to the side of him. The cop said something along the lines of, "Hey, Hoff, where ya been? Everyone's been looking for ya!" Then he stopped talking when the darkness of the room was illuminated by his flashlight. He realized that Hoff had a rope around his neck and that the rope had stretched over the past few days, giving off the appearance that his feet were touching the ground and that he was standing just the way a man would normally stand if he were still alive. The cop had been talking to a corpse.

We left the basement in search of higher floors. We saw what used to be the old wards where patients would have been in beds lined up in rows all together, and we saw what would have been private patient rooms (most of which are for nightly rentals as hotel rooms today). As we walked throughout the building, I couldn't help but notice that there were parts of the building that still smelled like an old hospital. It was a little unnerving.

Tom also pointed out many of the original details of the building that I thought were fascinating, such as the chutes to the incinerator and the nurse's call lights. The instructions on the chute door state, "Garbage must be thoroughly drained and wrapped in paper."

What sort of garbage requires thorough drainage? If you can't figure that one out, I can't help you. I saw cabinets containing old medical artifacts (along with bones) and even met the resident mascot. We were taken into the death rooms and up to the former psych ward and solarium.

The hallway of the Jerome Grand Hotel.

The solarium is gorgeous during the daytime, but when you are sitting there, you can't help but think about the fact that you are sitting in the former psych ward, and that the patients who came before you didn't sit on the sofa. They enjoyed the view while sitting in a three-point restraint chair, much like the mascot we met earlier.

The Mysterious Executive Who Shot Himself in Room 32

Room 32 (the room we stayed in) is believed to have been the site of two suicides while the hospital was in operation. A miner who had been confined to a wheelchair (and who was allegedly a known suicide risk because of this) somehow threw himself off the balcony. The other was a mine executive who shot himself in the head.

The mascot of the hotel is perched in a three-point restraint chair.

One of the patients rooms.

The solarium provides a gorgeous view of the area.

Tom told us that one female guest had recently run out of the room in her nightgown in the morning while she was getting ready to take a shower. She apparently saw something in the mirror and was very upset by what she saw. I don't know what the female guest saw in that mirror, but for some reason, the image that springs to mind is a man's face with a gaping gunshot wound through his head.

In Herbert Young's first book, *Ghosts of Cleopatra Hill*, he documents an obituary from November 22, 1932. It was for Thomas Taylor, and the news read:

> " ... one of the most colorful figures in the history of mining in the West died today at the United Verde Hospital in Jerome at the age of sixty-seven. His death followed a self-inflicted bullet wound. Mr. Taylor had been in poor health for some months past, having undergone a series of mouth operations in New York. Worn down by suffering, and evidently in the fear it might be necessary for him to undergo further operations, he performed the act which ended in his death."

Perhaps the executive thought to be lurking in room 32 is Thomas Taylor.

"Mary's" Room

Room 37B is referred to as "Mary's Room," and it is believed that a young woman was sent to the sanatorium part of the hospital by her family because she was suffering from schizophrenia. Guests have reported seeing a lady in white in this area and also have witnessed a figure sitting in one of the chairs who repeats, as though stuck in a loop, "I'm not schizophrenic."

A descendant of Gurthie May Patch contacted the hotel, and this relative provided a copy of her death certificate. Gurthie had leapt from her room (twenty-five feet in the air) in a suicide attempt and survived for thirty-six hours after the fall, eventually succumbing to the injuries she caused herself. Many believe that the spirit of Gurthie May Patch is associated with the hauntings in room 37B.

The Grand Suite and Former Operating Room

Today, the Grand Suite is the room behind the big windows in the front of the building that now has the "Jerome Grand Hotel" sign. This is the former operating room. While in town, we met a local (while we were researching in the library) who shared an interesting story about this room. The local said that when the Altherrs were preparing to open the hotel, they invited the townspeople up to walk through it one more time before they officially opened for business. She said that she went up with a male friend and when they walked into the operating room, her grounded, serious friend walked into a corner and dropped to the ground. A guy who never shut up suddenly grew quiet and began to cry. He looked up at her and said, "I died here." I would dismiss this as just a good story, but because of the similar experience I had in Eureka Springs, Arkansas, I believe this story. We also heard some stories about a nurse and a doctor when we struck up a conversation with another resident. One version went that a crazy nurse was killing babies by injecting them with blood thinners. The other version went that a nurse and a doctor who were having an affair were actually delivering babies that the "ladies of the night" in town kept having and then selling them to the rich families in town who were unable to have their own children. In case you are wondering, the proper response when someone tells you a story is to respond by saying, "Hmph! That's interesting!" Do this across the board as general policy and it will keep you out of trouble. I do not have an opinion about these stories because I have been unable to locate an actual witness as far as a former hospital employee that can substantiate them.

Again, using the vast power of social media, I tracked down some firsthand witness accounts of personal experiences that other people have had while staying at the hotel.

A Report from Jessica

When I got home, I connected with a woman named Jessica because I came across some photos she had posted online, and she was kind enough to share this heartwarming story that took place inside the clubhouse:

> In January of 2013 I was deployed to the Middle East. My mom contacted me via Facebook to inform me that my stepfather, who had raised me since I was ten, was being taken off life support. I was devastated and had very little time to digest this information. I called home, my mom was in his room, and she put the phone up to his ear so I could say my good-byes from halfway across the world. This was tough for me. We were very close. I named my first son after him. So, fast-forward to July, 2014. The day we had planned to go investigating was the same day I had decided to get a tattoo honoring my stepdad. We go investigating, not too much is happening, a little bit of the flashlight turning on and off in response to questions and what not, that was pretty cool. We started first, early in the evening on the top floor of the clubhouse, and then around 10:00 p.m. moved down to the 2nd Floor. When we were about to call it a night, my mom's friend decided to use her spirit box. The spirit had started with the flashlight and we came to the realization that we were speaking with my stepdad. He would only respond if my mom asked him a question. While the flashlight was going the spirit box was also. I asked my mom to ask if he heard me when I said good-bye over the phone (when I talked to him, he was in

a coma) ... loud and clear, without a doubt, "YES" came over the spirit box. We actually videotaped the whole encounter. Needless to say, there wasn't a dry eye in that room, there were about six of us there. He also said "smile" over the spirit box. Whether it was really his spirit or not, I will never know, but it gave me the closure I needed and let me get rid of the guilt that I felt for not being there. That night at the Old Clubhouse was a healing experience for me.

I believe whole-heartedly that sometimes those who have passed on do have the power to give us the peace we need.

Anonymous Report from Former Jerome Resident

Again utilizing social media, I located a witness (who wishes to remain anonymous) who came to Jerome by chance around 1976 with a friend when she was nineteen, staying until 1982. She did echo my experience about how it is weird how the town affects people. Some people don't want anything to do with the town, feeling the energy is bad, but some, like her, are drawn to it. During her time there, she worked as the town's first woman firefighter and stayed in the fourth hospital many times. She also helped restore the clubhouse. She knew Hoff and verified his suicide, stating that she was shocked to hear the news because he seemed like a happy guy.

She experienced many residual type hauntings, but the most notable instances were of being woken up by the sounds of screams. When she got up to explore and went outside, she actually saw an image of a person falling from the balcony, and she could see the outline of the person on the ground. She has also experienced the sounds of typewriters, drawers opening and closing, babies crying, the sounds of the elevator moving although it had been shut down, and the sound of a leg being dragged as though someone is walking with a limp. She also reported an intelligent haunting once when she was alone in a room, and her partner was across the building taking a shower. She felt heavy breathing behind her and thought it was her partner. When she turned around, nobody was there.

She had several other residual experiences in the town, including one very powerful past-life type experience that she referred to as a "bleed through." She was hiking to an old elevator mine shaft and suddenly began to feel very strange. She said she isn't sure what happened—if she walked into some kind of residual thing or what—but she looked down, and clear as day she saw herself wearing khaki pants and carrying a lunch pail. She was in miner's attire! She mentioned that the high concentration of copper could be acting as a conductor for all of this energy. That makes complete sense!

Reports from Kim Brasher

Kim is a frequent guest of the hotel and has had many overwhelmingly positive experiences while ghost hunting there. She has even developed relationships with a few of them. One is Michael, who she did not know while he was alive, but she has made contact with him in the after-life. Michael was squatting (camping out/trespassing) in the Clubhouse when he shot himself on the courthouse steps in the 1990s. Kim believes that Michael was able to cross over with the help from one of his friends who is still living and working in the Clubhouse building. They believe that he is able to go back and forth even after he crossed. There is one extremely helpful spirit that comes around and actually brings other spirits through to get messages to their loved ones. I agreed to keep his name confidential, but he did have ties to the area in life. Kim said that it has been happening more frequently where this spirit seems to be helping people get the closure they need by being able to reach their deceased relative or loved one. I think that is amazing!

While ghost hunting, they have had the voice of (someone who they believe is) a nurse come over their ghost box as though she is making a page for "Dr. Ernest." The lady in white who hangs around Rooms 31 and 33 has told her to "get the hell out." In room 37B, she had an experience where it seemed as though a bunch of children were in the room. The most fascinating story, in my opinion, is that when she was with a group one night, they seemed to be talking to the murderer of Claude Harvey. Apparently, the motive was jealousy over a nurse and Claude's job. The session communicated that Claude was murdered on the fourth floor. She has tried to reach Claude before, and the word "murdered" came over the ghost box.

We also talked about why the town and the hotel might both be so haunted. She mentioned that the activity seems to intensify when there is a rainstorm, and she also mentioned that the mining past seems to hold strong because of the geology of the land (all of the quartz and minerals). When discussing the suicides, she shared the opinion that drug and alcohol abusers are more susceptible to being manipulated by bad spirits.

Stone Tape Theory

We heard from a Sedona astrologer about the stone tape theory. He pointed out that the areas that surround old mining towns are known to have higher reporting rates for ghosts and even UFO sightings. He opined that the vibrations in the energy of the minerals (particularly in gold and silver) are thought to provide easier communications with what we refer to as the paranormal world. All of this was sounding familiar to me, but I could not recall the exact term until I picked up a copy of Zak Bagans's 2015 book, *I am Haunted: Living Life Through the Dead*. He quotes his first book (*Dark World*) and reminds readers about the stone tape theory. His explanation is concise and reads:

... certain natural materials can act like tape recorders and store the energies of the living. According to this theory, an event, usually one that involves a great deal of emotion or trauma, can somehow be captured in the stonework surrounding it and then replay it like a recording under certain conditions. For example, an apparition of a miner running down a tunnel yelling "Cave in!" could be an event that was recorded by the rocks themselves. (118)

Evening Sets In at the Jerome Grand Hotel

After an excellent dinner at the hotel's Asylum Restaurant, which is located in the former main lobby of the hospital, we went to our room to prepare for an evening alone in the hotel. The most touching (and most powerful) experience we had was in room 37B. We captured a thirty-minute flashlight video with my iPhone that I uploaded to YouTube (under my "Haunted Asylums, Prisons, and Sanatoriums" account). Prior to starting the video, I believe I established that the person knew about the deaths or suicides at the United Verde Hospital, that they were surprised to know that it was January 2015, and that they could see us. They also indicated that to them the place still looks like a hospital.

Here is a transcript for the intelligent conversation we believe we had with a former patient (note that a light turning itself on, via twisting the top of one of three flashlights lined up on the floor in response to a question, is believed to indicate a "yes" answer, per my instructions given upon commencing the session):

Me: Are you a patient here?

Response: flickers and then flashes on and off very strongly in a few series.

Are there other patients still here with you in the building?

Are there other patients still here in the building but not in the room with us?

Lights up.

Do you talk to each other? Are you friends?

Are you always in the hospital? You don't leave, and you are a patient here?

Lights up.

A lot of people I talk to don't realize they've died.

A series of three lights on and off, and then flickering lights.

[Bob wonders if this happens when they are actually talking to us.]

Flashlight turned on in the middle of talking about the hospital closing in 1950 and sitting empty until 1996.

Are you May?

Were you a patient in this room?

Lights up.

Were you a miner?

Did you have TB?

Polio?

Schizophrenia?

Childbirth?

Do you know why you're here?

Quick flicker, then full on light.

Do you know anybody else here?

Are you amongst strangers?

Lights up.

Do you wish that you could leave this hospital?

Is this your home?

Light flickers.

Can you tell me if you're happy here?

Lights up.

There is an After.

Lights up.

I think you're telling me that whatever you want to happen is
    what happens.

Lights up.

Is there anybody that you've looked for?

Lights up.

Are you waiting for someone to come find you and meet you here?

Have you ever loved anybody?

Lights up.

Are you still looking for that person?

Is your loved one here with you now?

Lights up.

Was your loved one a patient at this hospital too?

Is your loved one from Jerome?

How about Arizona?

Are you from Jerome?

Lights up.

Do you know Dr. Carlson?

Strong lights, in a series. This goes on for several seconds.

Do you think that he did a good job here?

Do you think that Dr. Carlson was a good doctor?

Do you think Dr. Carlson was a bad doctor?

What about the nurses?

Lights up before I get the full question out—has me wondering
*   if I'm getting a response to the question before about Carlson.*

Such a strong light, it's almost like you're trying to tell me
    Dr. Carlson did something bad.

Strong flickering on and off in response to that.

The experience left me worn out and exhausted, as it usually does, and we went to bed without event, sleeping soundly throughout the night. The next morning I sat in the sun on the balcony and enjoyed the view for about an hour while I read and wrote. The feeling was addictive to me, much like I felt about the third floor of the Old South Pittsburg Hospital in Tennessee several years ago. I felt like it was the best place in the world for me at that moment in time. I did not want to get up and leave. I could actually feel my body as though it was a battery and I was sitting on a charging station.

I am without a doubt convinced that there are intelligent souls knocking around inside that former hospital. For whatever reason, I got a good, protective one that left me feeling peaceful and hopeful about life and what comes after. I think that is what I found because that is what I wanted to find. I don't go into a place looking for the darkness. I don't want to further explore the dark side of humanity or seek out evidence of evil. I found out a long time ago that random evil exists in the world on a grand scale, and I really just don't want anything to do with it now. As I have aged, my tastes have changed and my idea of a good time has changed.

Now I just want to exist peacefully and not make or receive too much trouble. I want to read words that are new to me, eat good food under the sun, and enjoy the view. I want to experience the thrill of exploring a new city by foot, meet new people, and learn something new as often as possible. I did that here. I left energized and fulfilled. Admittedly, I also enjoy being up high and looking down on things. (Some experts in the past life regression field might argue that this is strong evidence that I am a former Princess or Queen. I'm certainly not going to argue about that.)

Comments from Bob

Every town has a certain feel or essence. Some are friendly and welcoming, some are bland and boring, some are sleepy and tranquil, and some are busy and driven. Some have their energy—scarcely noticeable—humming in the background. Then there is Jerome, Arizona, which has a strong dominant energy just beyond the range of the five senses. While the people of this town are charming, friendly, and warm, the town has a dark and ominous feel to it. It is hard to describe, but I felt very much like I was being watched. I could not tell whether I was being casually observed or actively watched through the scope of a rifle. If I were a dog, I would have been growling with my hackles up (or maybe hiding under the bed).

It is easy enough to blend in to the modern day Jerome with all the shops and restaurants, but lurking just beneath the surface is something from years gone by... something that refuses to let go. The theory that the underground copper is a good conductor of energy is a logical one. I also think that dark spirits can easily inhabit the bodies of people under the influence of alcohol and drugs. The myriad mysterious suicides might give credence to this theory. There seem to be many easy, if not willing, conduits in this town.

When we arrived at the Jerome Grand Hotel, I was very uncomfortable. There was an eerie presence. It didn't seem threatening, but we sensed something was very much there and very much aware of our presence. We immediately went exploring. I am of the opinion that just as a watched pot never boils, much paranormal activity happens to people not necessarily searching for it. The most credible stories happened to unwitting victims who were caught by surprise and deeply affected. Those going in search of the paranormal, I believe, possess a watchful consciousness that might block some of this activity. We went forward nonetheless.

One of the unnerving things about this hotel was this creepy "mascot," as Jamie called it. It is a very mentally disturbed looking characterization of a patient that sits in a three-point restraint seat in the hallway of the second floor of the hotel (across the hall from the Asylum Restaurant). It just sits gnawing its knuckles and staring through terrifying eyes. You know it is not a real person but you still don't want to get too close to it. You feel it staring at you when you walk down the hall. It adds to the ambiance of a haunted hotel with many stories to tell.

I am not sure what drove Hoff to commit suicide, but there was nothing during our visit that suggests his presence is still there. Claude Harvey met a tragic end, and while there has been considerable discussion as to whether he died in an accident or was murdered, there was nothing I saw that suggests his soul still haunts the premises. The K-II meter received many very hot readings in the stairwells, however, and there was something lighting up that flashlight.

As a neophyte guarded in my beliefs, I saw what I consider strong evidence of paranormal activity at the Jerome Grand Hotel. I saw a flashlight sit on the floor and light up seemingly all by itself over the course of a thirty-minute session that was captured on video. Whatever or whomever we were talking to seemed to have an actual consciousness and was cooperative and not unfriendly. In fact, it was a rather heartwarming "conversation." Immediately after the interview, we went to bed and there was no more perceptible activity.

I awoke the next morning and went to the lobby in search of hot coffee. The halls of the hotel seemed to have a calm and peaceful feel much different than when we arrived, like somehow we were vetted and found acceptable by the resident ghosts. That creepy little bastard sitting in the chair still freaked me out, though.

If You Decide to Visit

Location & Contact Info

200 Hill Street

Jerome, Arizona 86331

Tel: 928-634-8200

E-mail: *jghfrontdesk@yahoo.com*

Website: *http://www.jeromegrandhotel.net/*

Type of Tours & Hunts Offered

The ghost hunt and tour is sold as a package to hotel guests only. The cost is $30.00 per adult and $20.00 for children 12 & under. The tours are offered on select weeknights 6:00–7:30 p.m.

Size: Approximately 30,000 sq. ft.

Price: Rooms start at $155.00 per night for a Mountain View room.

Tips & Suggested Itinerary

Spring for a balcony room. The views are truly not to be missed! The Haunted Hamburger and the hotel's own Asylum Restaurant are my meal picks. The Gold King Mine Ghost Town is a photographer's dream. Visit the Douglas Mansion in the Jerome State Historic Park to learn all about mining and stand on glass over the 1,900 ft. Audrey Shaft.

Closest Airports

Flagstaff Pulliam Airport (FLG)—about 72 miles away

Phoenix Sky Harbor International Airport (PHX)—about 115 miles away

Tucson International Airport (TUS)—about 233 miles away

Las Vegas McCarran International Airport (LAS)—about 268 miles away

SEVEN

The Farnsworth House Inn
Gettysburg, PA

The Battle of Gettysburg ended on July 3, 1863. An estimated fifty-one thousand soldiers died, making this the largest battle ever fought in the United States. War undeniably left a stain on the land. The aftermath was horrific. For health reasons, crews swept the fields and buried thousands in shallow trenches. The Gettysburg National Military Blog reports that as late as 1995, archaeologists were still finding the remains of unidentified soldiers in shallow, unmarked graves. When you combine the horrors of war and the surprise and trauma of the nearly departed—who may not realize that they are dead—with undignified and unmarked graves, this is surely a recipe for some lingering spirits. For so many deaths to occur right at the same time could explain the amount of residual hauntings that visitors experience not just while walking through the battlefields, but throughout the town of Gettysburg itself. One of the most common occurrences for visitors is to witness residual imprints of soldiers reenacting battles, only to find out later that there were no reenactments scheduled to occur that day. It is as though you are watching a movie, and the residual imprints of the soldiers are playing on an endless loop.

I have read that the Battle of Gettysburg might even be responsible for the modern profession of funeral directors and embalmers. An article titled "Death and Mourning in the Civil War Era" tells of embalmers and funeral directors perfecting their trade out of necessity to deal with the volume of deaths and the distance of surviving family members. Embalming formulas had to be perfected in order for bodies to sustain the trip back home to be buried. Also, special coffins with viewing windows were constructed to aid families in recognizing their dead when trains carrying bodies pulled into town.

History

The Farnsworth House was very much in the center of 1863 Gettysburg and very much in the center of the fighting. The original part of the home was constructed in 1810, and the brick farmhouse structure was built in 1833.

The exterior of the Farnsworth House Inn.

According to the Farnsworth House Inn website, the house is "named in honor of Brigadier General Elon John Farnsworth, who led an ill-fated charge after the failure of Pickett's charge." An interesting fact is that the home was on the path of Lincoln's procession on November 19, 1863, when he was traveling to the National Cemetery to give the famous Gettysburg Address. The Farnsworth House also served as a hospital. When you walk around the home, look for the more than a hundred bullet holes that have marked the walls.

Now a bed and breakfast, the building is preserved in nearly the same condition as it was then.

Visiting the Farnsworth House

We stayed for two nights, staying in the Sara Black Room the first night, followed by a stay in the McFarlane Room. The interior of the home is fully outfitted in the style of the Victorian period.

The staircase of the Farnsworth.

The parlor of the Farnsworth.

The rooms contain a bedside journal where guests log their experiences (many are paranormal claims) while staying at the Farnsworth House Inn. The inn is thought to be the current home of fourteen different spirits. Some of the usual suspects include the following:

Jeremy
There is a story of a young lad named Jeremy who died in the Farnsworth House. The story goes that he was accidentally run over by a horse and carriage and then taken to the Sarah Black Room where he died. Jeremy is reported to be a very active ghost, and it is said that he has been seen in all of the rooms. He is often blamed for moving objects around.

There is a plaque on the wall inside the room that states the spirit of Jeremy's father can still be seen as a full-body apparition, appearing by the bedside throughout the night. Other guests staying in this room have written that they have heard what sounds like bodies being dragged across the floor of the attic (which is just above this room) and phantom pounding on the door to their room.

Late on the first night while staying in the Sara Black Room, we were talking and started laughing about something. While we were laughing, a little boy's disembodied laughter joined us out of nowhere! I ran to the window to look down at the street to see if we were hearing foot traffic below us, but there was no one outside. I flung open the door to our room and peered out into the hallway, but there were no other guests walking around. The next morning when we went down to breakfast, we met the other two guests that stayed in the main house the previous night. They were two brothers. There were no children staying at the Farnsworth House Inn that night. If we were hearing street noise, it seems unlikely that the child could have made it out of our line of vision by the time I ran to the window and looked out, but anything is certainly possible.

We began talking more with the brothers over breakfast. They considered themselves somewhat frequent guests at the house. One of them told us a story of a personal experience he had the last time he stayed in Jeremy's Room upstairs. He swore that one night he went to bed and left his keys and wallet on the bedside table. When he woke up the next morning, he found his keys scattered near the door. He couldn't explain that away.

There are different toys inside the Sara Black Room and some guests have written in the bedside journal that they have left the room or woken up in the morning to find that the set of toy letter blocks have arranged themselves while they were not looking to spell out messages to the guests: "Hi _____." If that happens to you, I do not know how to explain that away!

The Soldiers in the Attic and the Jennie Wade Connection

The Farnsworth House Inn has a very well documented and violent past. According to an article entitled "A Civil War Heroine," which ran in *The Western News* on December 25, 1901, Confederate sharpshooters took positions in the upper levels of the Farnsworth House and the adjacent buildings and fired on Union positions. One such position contained a civilian named Jennie Wade, a young lady from Ohio whose fiancée, a Union soldier, died in this battle. The story goes that Miss Wade was making biscuits for the hungry Union troops when a projectile from a common type of Confederate musket penetrated a wall, went into the kitchen, and struck her in the chest. Jennie Wade was the only civilian known to be killed in this battle, and the shot is thought to have been fired from a sharpshooter at the Farnsworth House. The attic is said to still hold the spirits of more than a few soldiers. One group is believed to be Confederate sharpshooters, and another is a solitary young soldier who still mans his post, a post he held and was told not to relinquish—and still hasn't. You might even hear him say, "I was ordered to stay put." The sharpshooters were apparently working under an assembly line type of strategy. If the shooter in front of you was hit by gunfire and killed, the men behind him simply dragged his body over to the corner of the attic and the next shooter stepped up to take his turn in the firing squad.

The attic used to be rented out as a bed and breakfast room, but too many people were upset by their experiences, so it became regulated just for tours. Allegedly, guests were waking up to full-body apparitions of soldiers who were talking; guests were hearing musical instruments when there shouldn't be any sounds; and guests were hearing phantom footsteps coming all the way to the edge of the bed they were trying to sleep in.

The Midwife

Other stories tell of a woman whose apparition is preceded by a very strong smell of gardenias, a flower commonly used in funerals. She is believed to be the spirit of a midwife who helped a woman deliver a stillborn baby in one of the rooms. A strong feeling of sadness is said to be present in that room, and this apparition will appear when a guest is very sad or feeling ill, usually preceded by the smell of gardenias.

While researching for this chapter, I was fortunate to discover the blog of Jennifer Melzer, an author, poet, and editor from Northern Pennsylvania who was kind enough to share her personal experiences while staying at the Farnsworth House Inn. Her story in her own words is as follows:

> In 2012 my husband James and I booked the Sara Black Room at the historic Farnsworth House Inn in Gettysburg, Pennsylvania. We chose the Sara Black Room because stories claimed a little boy named Jeremy died in that room after he was trampled by a horse in the streets out front. There were tons of toys in the room: blocks, balls, and little soldiers, and the staff claimed leaving them out for him to play with might prompt him to interact. As soon as we arrived, James laid out balls, set up soldiers and used the lettered blocks to spell out the words HI JEREMY. We set up our video camera in the corner, and then went to lunch at Sweeney's Tavern downstairs.
>
> We did not capture anything on video. The camera, which was fully charged when we left, was drained when we returned about an hour later. None of the toys moved during our absence. I was disappointed, but I was starting to get more annoyed with the obnoxious children from the fine dining restaurant downstairs and the parents allowing them to run roughshod through the Inn. There weren't supposed to be children in the bed and breakfast, and their playful stomping and laughter was going to get old quickly.
>
> We were later told there were no families in the restaurant downstairs. In fact, there were no customers at all. This seemed like our first encounter with the ghost children of the Farnsworth House Inn, but the excitement didn't stop there.

While on the phone, someone came to our bedroom door and tried to open it. They jiggled the handle and pushed against the frame, but when my husband went to see who was there, the hallway was empty.

At 9 p.m. we took the guided house tour. Part of the tour took place in the attic, which just so happens to be right above the Sara Black Room. Our guide claimed we might hear heavy boots stomping across the floor, the dragging of bodies, coughs, murmurs, and whispers. I could live with that, but when we descended into the basement, I felt every hair on my body rise.

According to our guide, someone broke the rules a few years earlier and brought a Ouija board into the inn. They invited a malevolent spirit into the Farnsworth, and though a professional had trapped it to keep it from harming someone, you could actually feel its presence. It was November, so I expected it to be chilly, but the air in that room was cold in ways I can't put into words.

I felt physically and emotionally relieved when we left the cellar, but it felt as if the energy itself clung to me when we headed back upstairs for what promised to be a sleepless night.

To warm the chill from my bones, I decided to relax in the claw-foot tub, but as soon as I stretched out, my husband came barreling into the bathroom to tell me about the bed mysteriously shaking as though someone kicked the posts and frame. I don't know how I thought we were going to get any sleep in that place. By the time we crawled into bed, leaving the small light in the bathroom on like eight-year-olds hiding under the covers from monsters, the sound of heavy boots thumping across the floor accompanied the promised dragging and loud *whoomphs* that could only be described as bodies being tossed into piles.

We heard men's voices, quiet and muffled, and every time they spoke my entire body tingled. It was so unnerving we barely slept. We did try to set up video and audio each time we left the room, but the batteries always drained and died shortly after we departed. Only once did the audio manage to run the whole time we were gone. It picked up the sound of the closet door opening and closing multiple times, which gave me chills because the same closet door popped open a lot while we were in the room during the day. Whenever we closed it, it wouldn't stay closed.

We didn't see any physical evidence during our stay. None of the toys we set out for Jeremy moved, we never caught anything on video, and the volumes of photographs we took didn't have anything strange or inexplicable in them, but there was plenty of atmospheric evidence to convince me there was definitely something paranormal going on at the Farnsworth House Inn.

I also heard from Cyndi Vojvoda, the founder of a paranormal group based in the Chicago suburbs called Hunters of the Unknown. She is a registered nurse by day and a paranormal investigator by night. Here is what she had to say about visiting the Farnsworth House Inn:

Gettysburg is a graveyard for the multitude of souls killed on this land. The second I stepped foot in town it felt like I was in a different time. There was a heavy, oppressing feel, like a dark cloud covered this historical town, which is understandable considering the tens of thousands of deaths that happened here.

I stayed two sleepless nights in the McFarlane Room of the Farnsworth House Inn. This room was decorated beautifully, but because of the dark shades of purple on the walls and furniture, the room felt like a dungeon, even with the lights on. Antique children's clothes hung on the walls. I had to take these off the wall and store them in the bathroom to even attempt to sleep.

Being a paranormal investigator, I brought a couple devices to determine if there were indeed spirits in this Inn. I did a sweep of the room with an EMF meter, a device that detects electromagnetic fields, which some believe spirits give off. I received a response near the floor but concluded there could be wires or pipes running through the floor causing it to give a false reading. I conducted an EVP session in which you ask questions to the spirits in hopes of recording a response on an audio recorder, but did not receive a reply. Despite the fact there is nothing above the McFarlane Room, I heard footsteps above but also concluded this sound could be coming from someone walking in the hall, the sounds echoing throughout the building. I took a local ghost tour that ended in the attic of the Farnsworth House Inn. While the tour guide was telling stories of the history of the building, the attic door mysteriously opened on its own. The building is very old. Floors could be uneven, doors warped. The door might have swung open for no paranormal reason. I feel I did not obtain any concrete proof of spirits residing in the Farnsworth House Inn, only an ominous feeling.

It would be very easy to say some of these experiences were paranormal. After all, I knew I was staying in a place that was rumored to be haunted and expected to have a personal experience with the ghosts that inhabit this Inn. I think people who stay here have the expectation they will encounter something paranormal, but ghosts don't appear on demand. The entire town of Gettysburg was one of the battlefields for the Civil War, no wonder the town felt creepy.

Investigating and Exploring the Cellar

The cellar, used primarily as a theater, is said to be a very active place, with reports ranging from full-body apparitions to shadow people darting around. We spent some time there investigating after breakfast our first morning so we could have some time alone in the area. The Farnsworth House Inn has very narrow, winding hallways that are almost carnival-like when you are twisting and turning to walk through them. When we were descending the basement stairs to investigate the cellar on our own, we did so in total darkness.

While in the basement, we operated only with the illumination provided by our cell phones (really eerie!) until Bob later found the light switch when we were preparing to leave the area. Our photos will reveal why we were glad to get back upstairs.

There are many varied and original artifacts from the Victorian era in this basement. In an article on the Farnsworth House Inn, Rene Staub, the marketing manager at the Farnsworth House Inn, discusses some of the artifacts that are kept on display at the home. It made me consider whether there is a possibility of any spirit attachments to any of these historic artifacts and if this could be a reason for many of the hauntings in the home.

The Hair Wreaths

When I happened upon the authentic hair wreaths by the light of my iPhone, I was a little taken aback. Many of the props in the theater are just that, props used to set the mood or the stage, so to speak. However, there are apparently some real pieces of Victorian mourning artifacts housed in the cellar of the Farnsworth House Inn. I have only seen one other hair wreath in my life, and it was in a plantation museum in Washington, Georgia. Traditionally, when a relative died, a surviving family member cut off a piece of the deceased's hair and sewed it into the family wreath and hung it on the wall like that was a totally normal piece of art.

The basement of the Farnsworth is set up for haunted lectures.

A doll peeks out of a coffin at the back of the Farnsworth's basement.

A casket adorned with flowers and candles is at center
stage in the basement of the Farnsworth.

This was a way for the family to remember their loved one, and this was especially the case if they could not afford the expense of photography. The Victorians were also fond of using hair in jewelry. Now, as a Southerner, I can tell you that it is not at all uncommon to clip a lock of hair from a dead relative and keep it in a locket or a jewelry box. For one thing, you never know when you might need it later, but we do not keep these artifacts on display in our homes anymore. Those wreaths are just creepy! I have no idea what sort of weird residual attachments might go along with having that amount of strange, dead human hair stored in one place that has so many deaths and tragedies connected to it.

The Victorian period lasted from 1837 to 1901, and many of the mourning customs (at least the fashion part of it) came from Queen Victoria when she lost her husband. The Victorians were known for being romantic and sentimental, but from my reading, I am not sure if that was necessarily the case. In any event, wandering around the cellar certainly inspired me to think about many of the Victorian funeral rituals and mourning customs.

Post-Mortem Photography

This old mourning custom ranks right up there with hair wreaths as far as the creep factor. The invention of photography only predated the Battle of Gettysburg by about twenty years, so for most Americans, photography was an extremely expensive innovation, and they only used it to document a death (as the deceased likely would never have had a prior photo taken). It would not have been at all uncommon to see a photo of the deceased posed just like they were alive—with props such as a gun if he was a soldier, or if a child, sitting up around a pile of toys. You can usually tell by the eyes. Many times the eyes look like glass replacements, or they would be manually secured open via sewing jobs. Sometimes the photographer would go back later and fix the eyes in the photo by painting over them.

Cover the Mirrors and the Portraits. Stop the Clocks!

Traditionally, there was a fear of mirrors and portraits being portals. The family made sure to cover the mirrors so the spirit of the deceased wouldn't get trapped inside. Survivors would also take care to cover the family portraits so that the deceased wouldn't be able to possess them. If there was a clock in the room or house, it was to be stopped at the time of death because it was thought to ward off bad luck, and this was also done out of respect for the deceased to symbolize time standing still until they could be laid to rest. Stopping clocks is still done in the South to this day. There is a practical reason, of course, because it helps the coroner pinpoint the exact time of death, but there is a deep tradition and respect to it as well.

While we have nothing to report from our time in the cellar, it still left me in deep need of some fresh air, so we headed over to spend the afternoon at the Gettysburg National Military Park.

Comments from Bob

After a magnificent video and cyclorama presentation at the visitor center, we drove ourselves on a guided tour of the park by car. We were looking for a secluded place to sit, listen, and be still. We found just the spot at the base of Devil's Den, one of the locations of the heaviest sniper fire during the Battle of Gettysburg. This location changed hands three times during the three days of battle and the casualties there were very heavy.

While the area was very serene on this drizzly morning in May, Jamie and I sat for almost thirty minutes and both heard very faint sounds of distant cannon fire, being carried on the wind. We checked and found there were no cannon firings anywhere near Gettysburg on that day. Later that evening, at dusk, which is known to be a very charged time paranormally, we found another secluded location around the same area and heard the sounds of horses' hooves. A search of the area revealed no horses in the proximity. The sounds did not seem normal, but had a hollow distance to them, like ethereal echoes of days long past.

Were these sounds really there? Are there residual echoes from a very intense battle that are still carried on the winds? Or could the battle still be raging in another dimension at the edge of ours? On the surface, the town of Gettysburg and nearby battlefields, around which the Farnsworth House Inn is nestled, seem very much at peace and at rest. Could there be more going on here?

We report, you decide.

If You Decide to Visit

Location & Contact Info

401 Baltimore Street

Gettysburg, Pennsylvania 17325

Tel: 717-334-8838

E-mail: *info@farnsworthhouseinn.com*

Website: *http://www.farnsworthhouseinn.com*

Type of Tours & Hunts Offered

Ghost tours and hunts nightly; Deluxe Paranormal nights twice a month

Size: 10 rooms

Price: starting at $135.00 per night

Tips & Suggested Itinerary

Gettysburg is a town and national park area that should be on every American's bucket list. The Farnsworth House Inn has a tavern and dining room on-site, but we also enjoyed visiting the historic 1776 Dobbin House Tavern for dinner. Be sure to stop by the Jennie Wade House, and reserve an entire day for the battlefield and visitor center. There are many ghost walks and tours to choose from when the sun goes down, but if you only have one night in town, Bob and I highly recommend that you just spend some time on your own in a part of the field that draws you. Sit quietly and listen. You will probably be surprised by what you hear out there!

Closest Airports

Harrisburg International Airport (MDT)—about 47 miles away

Baltimore/Washington International Thurgood Marshall Airport
  (BWI)—about 61 miles away

Washington Dulles International Airport (IAD)—about 78 miles away

Ronald Reagan Washington National Airport (DCA)—
about 88 miles away

EIGHT

The Lemp Mansion
St. Louis, MO

Stephen P. Walker's *Lemp: The Haunting History* recounts the family's beer baron story. The tale of the Lemp family in America began with Johann Adam Lemp, who came from Germany in 1836. Johann was the proprietor of a grocery store in St. Louis and shortly began brewing lager beer as well (there is some dispute as to whether he was the first or second person to brew lager beer in America, but he was most certainly the first person to do so in St. Louis). He was so successful that he abandoned the grocery store to develop his brewery business. He found a natural cave and used it to store his beer. Johann died on August 23, 1862, and the business passed to his only son, William J. Lemp. William built the Lemp Brewery as we know it today, and Walker wrote that he chose this site because it was where his father had already established his caves. By 1877, William was operating the biggest brewery in the city and was ranked nineteenth in the country. He also acquired his own railroad (Western Cable Railway Company) for use in transporting beer. It has been widely reported that Lemp ran pipes from the brewery all the way into his home so that he could serve his beer from taps while relaxing at home.

William Lemp married Julia Feickert in 1861 and the Lemp Mansion was built in 1868, either by or for his in-laws (depending on who is telling the story). William and Julia purchased the home in 1876. They had nine children, the first of which was an infant who died in 1862. The other children were as follows: Anna (1865–1939); William J. Lemp, Jr. ("Billy," 1867–1922); Louis (1870–1931); Charles (1871–1949); Frederick (1873–1901); Hilda (1875–1951); Edwin (1880–1970); and Elsa (1883–1920). By all accounts, Frederick was the favorite child, and when he died on December 12, 1901, of heart failure at the age of twenty-eight, his father was completely shattered. William lost his best friend, Frederick Pabst, three years later on January 1, 1904. He was never the same after these two losses, and he committed suicide in the home on February 13, 1904. Julia died of cancer in the home in March 1906.

Billy took over the brewery after William's death. He had a well-publicized divorce from Lillian Handlan (the "Lavender Lady") in 1909, and both of them disclosed some very salacious arguments to say the least. Walker supplied my favorite quote, which came directly out of Billy's mouth during the trial, and helps demonstrate what a very different lifestyle the very rich lived compared with the working class: "Time and again, I came home and the meals were not ready. Often she would leave the house with the boy and give the servants no instructions regarding meals for me." Personally, it has always agitated me greatly when the servants can't get it together and have my meals at the table on time.

In 1911 the Lemp Mansion was converted into offices for the brewery and no one was living there any longer. In 1919 production abruptly stopped. Essentially, Prohibition killed the Lemp Brewery.

The exterior of the Lemp Mansion.

It was reported that the family members were all individually wealthy and did not care to fight any longer for their business. On March 19, 1920, Elsa allegedly committed suicide in her home at 13 Hortense Place.

The business was valued at seven million dollars in 1919, but Billy was only able to get $585,000 when he sold it to the International Shoe Company on June 28, 1922. Billy reportedly committed suicide in the home on December 29, 1922.

Charles moved back into the Lemp Mansion in 1929. Charles committed suicide in the home on May 10, 1949. He was seventy, arthritic, and in otherwise very poor health.

From the 1950s to the early 1970s, the home was operated as a boarding house. The Pointer family purchased the home in 1975, and the home is currently still in their hands.

Cherokee Caves

In *Down in the Darkness*, Troy Taylor points out that St. Louis is built on top of natural caves. In fact, he wrote, "no other city on earth has as many caves beneath its streets, sidewalks, and buildings." Once again I accidentally stumble upon another strange place that just happens to have miles of tunnels snaking underneath the surface! Although they are not accessible to the public anymore, there are plenty of online accounts from urban explorers who have found their way into this cave system. The entrance that used to lead from the Lemp Mansion itself into the brewery has long been sealed. The Lemp family used some of the cave space for a private swimming pool (referred to a little less glamorously today as a mere cement wading pool that was originally just a run-off for melting ice used to keep the beer cool—nothing luxurious whatsoever). The family also used some of the cave space for a theater. This sounds like a made-up story, but it isn't! Why in the world would someone want to watch a performance in one of these caves?! It really makes you wonder what was going on down there.

Witness Reports

Before we traveled, I sent many inquiries to different paranormal teams in the Missouri area in an attempt to get the scoop on the famous haunt. No other location that I have ever inquired about has inspired such controversy. I received many responses cautioning me about the alleged haunted happenings at the Lemp Mansion. Some of these negative responses came from a group of people that were apparently ticked off that the owners failed to allow them unfettered access to the home (without booking all of the rooms to cover the lost revenue opportunities) for a period of days to investigate the hauntings.

The other side of that coin is that I received reports from many other people attesting that they experienced a haunting while staying at the home.

A Report from Bobby Adams

Myself, my wife, and two other couples, all members of PRIMO (Paranormal Research and Investigations of Missouri), arrived Friday evening, August 2, 2013, looking forward to a night of rest and maybe adventure. Little did we know the "adventure" that was waiting for some of us. The group assembled in the Lavender Suite to plan our investigation. We decided to start on the ground floor and work our way up. We had to wait until the bar closed and all the staff had gone home to start our investigation. First, we placed multiple cameras and multiple digital voice recorders in multiple rooms. Second, we paired up in groups of two and started walking from room to room, starting in the kitchen and bar, and working our way upstairs to the attic rooms. As one team would investigate the rooms, the rest of us would remain quiet in another part of the house to keep down any audio interference.

As we moved from room to room we didn't detect any paranormal activity. Sure, we heard the occasional pop or cracking sound, but we attributed this to temperature changes within the building. We heard footsteps in other rooms; these footsteps were from other people who occupied rooms on the top floor. When all three teams had finished their investigations, we decided to call it a night and get some sleep.

We arose Saturday morning and assembled in the Lavender Suite for coffee and Danish. After breakfast, it was time to pack up and go home. I told my wife I was leaving to take as much gear as I could to the car and I would be right back. I grabbed as many bags as possible and headed toward the door. I took one step toward the door when from my left side I saw a full-bodied apparition of William Lemp. I recognized him from his pictures in the house. He was in a business suit and holding a letter. He walked right past me while looking at the sheet of paper. I watched him walk down the hall, then turn and enter a room with a locked door. I was in a state of shock and anger at the same time. Shocked at what I had just seen, and angry because my camera gear was packed away. RATS. Murphy's Law strikes again! Before we left the mansion, I told everyone who I saw. My team member asked, "Did you get it on film?" I said, "No, thanks to Murphy's Law." This was my experience at the Lemp Mansion.

A Report from Nikki Sweets

My experiences at the Lemp Mansion began during my first haunted history tour back in 1995, and occurred almost every single time I was there. Some experiences were more noticeable or exciting than others, but every visit was a treat. I always learned something new about the family or the house. I recall that my first visit was relatively uneventful, except for a short, cool breeze in an upstairs hallway as if a person walked by... but there was no person to be seen. During the "darkroom" sessions in the attic, I, as well as many others in the tour group, could see mists or balls of light in the dark at times. They seemed to have an intelligence about them as they moved around the visitors. That was pretty cool. I started going on the tours on a regular basis and was asked if I wanted to volunteer or help out during the tours for a few nights.

I helped out just a few times, but I learned so much. On one of the nights, I witnessed a bedroom door close by itself, then another bedroom door opened as I was approaching it.

I said, "Excuse me," as if there was a person coming into the room and I was in the way. By the time I got to the entranceway, there was nobody on the other side of that door opening it. I thought that was pretty amazing. On another night, I was sitting in a dining room (the room to the left of the front door when you enter) and although I was looking toward the window, I saw, out of the corner of my eye, a tall, nicely dressed man standing by the staircase. When I turned and looked at the staircase with both eyes, there was nobody there. Now that was pretty amazing!

Puzzling at first, the more things I saw out of the corner of my eye and heard others talk about the same thing, I realized I wasn't imagining it. Almost every visit had an experience, even if it was something so small as a shadow that occurred without a human body to create it. I do believe the Lemp Mansion is very haunted, but nothing about that house scares me. I believe that whatever entities are there, they are there because of love or because they feel a sense of comfort being there. I look forward to going back for an actual investigation with the St. Louis Paranormal Research Society, since I have learned more about collecting evidence over the years. I always encouraged people to visit the mansion and even stay there, because it is beautiful, rich in history, and they just might get an experience or two that they can't explain!

Visiting Lemp Mansion

A *Life Magazine* article that ran in November 1980 included the Lemp Mansion in its roundup of most haunted houses in America. The Pointer family reported many strange occurrences that happened in the home in the late 1970s during renovations. Full-bodied apparitions have been reported throughout the home, and staff members have reported glasses levitating in the bar.

After I got settled in to our attic Frederick and Louis Lemp Suite, I spent some time walking the house by myself and decided I liked the former library—now the bar, and possibly the room where Charles Lemp committed suicide in 1949, according to our tour guide—the best out of all the rooms.

I would return to it later that evening. In 2001, the Pointers had two stained-glass windows put in that were made in the image of Billy Lemp and his first wife, Lillian. I sat there for a few minutes and felt the stillness and quiet of the house.

The stained-glass window featuring Billy Lemp.

The stained-glass window featuring Lillian Lemp.

It was late afternoon, and the way the light was coming into the room, coupled with the stillness, reminded me of the day my grandfather died.

I remember how quiet the house was, and I think someone may have even stopped the clocks. Nothing was going on inside—we were out of time, but outside noise could still be heard. Birds continued to chirp and the guy across the street was outside mowing his lawn. The world didn't stop. The neighbor didn't even stop.

The harshest and cruelest part of death is realizing that nobody really cares outside of a handful of people. The world is so large that it won't be stopped by the death of one person ever again.

I think this is why the world has seen a shift back to the popularity of the paranormal once more. People are searching for meaning. They want to know that there is something else.

The Lemp Mansion was tomb-like and gothically dark inside on the afternoon of my visit. Yet cars whizzed by on Highway 55 mere feet away from the rear of the house. The world had stopped inside, but others were continuing to move forward.

The atrium and ceiling of the parlor were two distinct features of the house that were timelessly beautiful.

After I had explored the house, we walked the neighborhood. Today, the Lemp Brewery is a privately owned office and industrial complex. You can walk around the perimeter, of course, along the sidewalks, but there are "No Trespassing" and "No Photography" signs scattered throughout the complex. There is a haunted attraction company that rents space for the Halloween season and includes tours of a small part of the famous Cherokee Cave system for those of you who are curiosity seekers.

We booked a Monday night stay so we could take advantage of one of the haunted history tours. The St. Louis Spirit Search is the home paranormal team out at the Lemp Mansion.

The ceiling of Lemp Mansion's parlor.

They had a great setup in the front parlor with two tables covered with backboards that contained news articles and photos of the family. They also had several pairs of dowsing rods.

We sat downstairs for a good hour-and-a-half lecture that covered the history of the family and the home before we ever started moving throughout the house. Our guide talked about spirit guides being with each of us, which I thought was compelling because I had never heard anyone giving a tour say something like that before.

She went on to tell us about her roster of characters that she believes are still in the home in spirit form. She put the count at nine. There are even stories of ghost animals at Lemp—tales that revolve around Cerva, Charles Lemp's prized pet dog, in particular.

The Lemp Brewery is located near the mansion.

The legends claim that he shot his dog, a German Shepherd named Cerva, but I was unable to determine definitively whether or not this was the case.

The Lemp suicides were all heavily covered in the news of the day. On February 18, 1904, the *Iron County Register* covered the death of William J. Lemp in an article entitled "William J. Lemp a Suicide." The headline read, "The Well-Known St. Louis Brewer Kills Himself by Shooting. Grief over the Recent Death of His Son Edward the Supposed Cause of the Act." It was reported that he got up on Saturday morning (February 13), ate his breakfast, and then went back upstairs to his room. About an hour later, a shot rang out and he was found "in the throes of death. He was partially disrobed, and lay upon the bed with his revolver smoking on the blood-stained covers.

The man's muscles twitched, he breathed heavily. A gaping wound in his temple told the story ... Dr. Harmisch was the first to arrive. 'He is beyond all medical or surgical aid,' the doctor stated. At 10 o'clock he passed away."

Of note is that the historical records at the Lemp Mansion show that the son was named Frederick, not Edward. The Missouri History Museum goes further to provide that Frederick was the known favorite, who died of heart failure on December 12, 1901, at the age of twenty-nine. Other news articles and books also refer to Frederick as well. News stories simply do not always get it right!

Elsa Lemp's suicide followed on March 20, 1920. Elsa made news in the *New York Tribune* on Sunday, March 21, 1920, via a news article entitled "Heiress, Rewed 2 Weeks Ago, Kills Herself." The headline continues, "Mrs. Elsa Lemp Wright, Daughter of Late St. Louis Brewer, Fires Bullet Into Her Chest at Her Home." According to the article, Elsa died at her home located at 33 Westmoreland Place. She first married Thomas A. Wright in 1909 and divorced him in 1918, alleging that he had quit loving her and that he had "destroyed her peace and happiness." She claimed that he caused her to have a nervous breakdown. Then, she married Mr. Wright again about a year after the divorce. Mr. Wright did not make a comment about why his wife would have taken her own life. Much speculation has resulted from Elsa's death. It has been alleged that there was a large lapse in time from her body being discovered to the time when police were called to the scene. In fact, Troy Taylor has written that the first call Thomas Wright made was to his lawyer. However, her brothers did not make anything of it at the time, and Billy is famously quoted as saying, "That's the Lemp family for you."

Rebecca Pittman's 2015 book, *The History & Haunting of Lemp Mansion*, examines Elsa's death at length, arranging modern police detectives to review the entire file. Pittman even published Deputy Dever's coroner report.

There still remains a mystery around Elsa's death. Her husband, by his own testimony, heard the gunshot and found Elsa still alive in bed at 8:05 a.m. Initially, one of the maids testified that she heard these shots as well, although she would later go silent on this fact. Mr. Wright made his first call to his lawyer at 8:30 a.m. It is not clear what he was doing in the twenty-five minute time lapse from 8:05 to 8:30 a.m., other than watching Elsa and letting her die. The other circumstance that appeared suspicious to me is the gun was found on the couch in the bedroom, across the room from where Elsa was in the bed. Wright testified that he must have moved the weapon but could not remember doing so. Pittman's modern detective said that it is actually quite common for family members to move the weapon when they first discover the body. He also pointed out that if Mr. Wright was hiding anything, it's more likely that he would have left the gun positioned near Elsa's body instead of letting the police discover it over on the couch. Lastly, and perhaps the most suspicious of all the extenuating circumstances, Wright's lawyer called in a circuit judge, attorney, and the circuit court clerk before any public officials were notified. It sure would seem that he was controlling the scene, and when the deputy coroner got there, he had six jurors view Elsa's body and sign a blank verdict form. Later, he conducted the very brief witness interviews, filled in the verdict form, and made the official determination that ruled Elsa's death a suicide. Game over and case closed. We will never know what happened that morning.

According to Taylor in *Suicide & Spirits*, Elsa had befriended a woman named Pearl Currant and the two of them were very much involved in the spiritualism movement.

They held several séances in the mansion and apparently spoke with a spirit they called Patience Worth by using a Ouija board. Could the two of them have opened up something during these séances that remains inside the home today? It is a point worth considering.

*The Lavender Suite is dominated by the portrait
of Lillian Lemp, known as the Lavender Lady.*

The Topeka State Journal covered the third suicide in the family, that of William J. Lemp, Jr., on December 29, 1922. In "Brewer a Suicide," *The Topeka State Journal* headlines that "William J. Lemp Shoots Self Twice Thru the Heart." It was reported that Billy killed himself at the age of fifty-four because of ailing health and the great financial loss that came from selling the brewery for what amounted to eight cents out of a dollar.

At this point, Billy had turned the Lemp Mansion into offices. His secretary, Miss Bershek, heard the two gunshots. He was found on his back with a .38 caliber revolver beside him near his right hand.

The fourth suicide in the family was Charles A. Lemp, who was seventy-seven when he shot himself on May 10, 1949. Of all the Lemps, Charles was the single soul to leave a note. Charles did not mince words. He wrote: "In case I am found dead, blame it on no one but me."

Prior to beginning the dowsing rod session, our guide told us that she feels closest to the spirit of Billy and that she is frequently in contact with him. We were also reminded that we were sitting in the room where the funerals were held after the suicides of William and Billy Lemp. During the session, she said that something was there that was over-powering or making Billy uncomfortable. She looked up at us and said: "Airplane propellers. I'm getting airplane propellers." I am by no means an expert, but her hands were not moving those rods. Her body was completely still, yet the rods would cross, seemingly in response to her questions.

We moved into the next room, today called the Lavender Suite, which was the office where Billy shot himself. The painting of the Lavender Lady is a modern creation of Lillian Lemp, Billy's first wife, and not an original antique. In fact, Lillian never actually lived in this house. While talking to us, our guide thought she saw someone in white go up the stairs. We were all facing her at the time, so no one on the tour saw anything.

The second floor hallway of the Lemp Mansion.

The house was kept fairly dark throughout the tour, and we made our way upstairs to the second floor of the home and entered the William Lemp Suite. Once we were all gathered around the bed (and approximate suicide site of William Lemp), the guide asked us if we could smell a faint perfume smell. No one did. She also told us that Julia died in the room next door of cancer. Several EVPs were played for us.

The Dark Room Experience at Lemp Mansion

When we made it to the third floor via the servants staircase and inside the Louis Suite, our guide unlocked the door to the eaves, which is the attic area that winds around the outside of that wing of the home and has windows down to the street.

We all had a grand time exploring the unfinished part of the home. Once we had our fill of wandering, we shut the lights off in the room and began the Dark Room Experience. The guide told us the story of Zeke. It began with a preface that the house does not have any evidence on file of such a person existing (this means we are entering into story time, ladies and gentlemen).

Zeke was allegedly the tenth child of William and Julia Lemp and was kept in the attic because he was either physically or mentally disabled. Andrew Lemp Paulsen, who says he is the great-great-grandson of Anna Lemp Konta (first child of William and Julia Lemp), commented in the *Riverfront Times* on October 25, 2012, about the existence of Zeke. Paulsen said, "It's bogus. He never existed" (*Greenbaum*). The article then goes on to pinpoint the origination of the Zeke legend to a psychic who visited the home in the 1970s and claimed that the boy died in the home from a fall downstairs in 1943.

We all sat or stood in complete silence as our guide then called Cerva to us to see if the phantom dog would run in the room and say hello to us. She also asked me if I had felt a feeling of oppression when I first went into the room. I answered that I had not.

We sat there for several minutes, and our guide called and called—even pleading with Charles to let Cerva come visit. But the clock ticked forward, and Cerva did not come when called.

In closing, I thought it was a superior tour for what it was, which was entertainment for the night in a beautiful mansion with some very macabre, verifiable history. I do not know if our guide was really communicating with someone downstairs in the parlor using dowsing rods, and I don't know if she really saw a ghostly figure dash up the stairs, smelled a phantom perfume smell, or truly believed that a ghostly dog was going to visit us upstairs in the Louis Suite.

All of that is on her. She gave her customers a good experience and a night out in St. Louis on a dreary Monday, and everyone seemed satisfied by the experience. Everything that was presented as truth during the tour was backed up with displayed documents downstairs in the home, and it was made perfectly clear to those who were listening when she was reciting facts versus telling a scary story in the dark.

Granted we flew in for the night and were gone in the morning, we were just not able to spend two days alone inside the Lemp Mansion on this trip. There are plenty of people who have reported strange occurrences, but we just don't have one for you this time.

Sitting in the Bar

After the tour, people started to scatter and Bob and I made our way to the only dark area of the house, which was the bar (former library). While we did not have any paranormal experiences per se inside the Lemp Mansion on our visit, I did sit in the dark in the bar and have a sort of "Dark Night of the Soul" experience.

Inside my brain at the bar at Lemp Mansion: "Everything I do, did, and will ever do is just a waste of time. I don't understand why I'm even sitting here in this house right now.

There is no point in anything. I used to have so much fun. I hate everything now. I'm just so tired. I just want to be someone else, somewhere else. I am so sick and tired of doing all these things that no one even cares about."

Billy. I know why you did it.

Comments from Bob

Due to some complications with flights, I arrived in St. Louis a few hours before Jamie and was able to check in and see the Lemp Mansion. I always try to minimize any power of suggestion potential when we arrive at a supposed haunted place. Since I disdain official tours (after working in public affairs I know the official story is usually sanitized for public consumption), I rarely give any credence to what others are telling me. I try to use my senses and intuition to try to get an accurate feeling. (I used to drive the teachers and preachers nuts because I had to prove things to myself.)

Haunted places always seem to come with official folklore and tall tales. Many seem regurgitated and stale, and that is one reason I tend to disdain these tales. I wonder, however, if there is a reason for this and I wonder if one reason is to protect the actual spirits that inhabit a building or site. Perhaps the buildings owners are aware of a spirit that lives there but out of respect for the spirit want to protect that spirit. After all, like you and me, this spirit is a human soul. Perhaps earthbound, either by choice or circumstance, this soul inhabits this location. Can you imagine a worse fate than to have people come into this ghost's presence regularly and try to get him to do fun ghost things? People love monkeys at a zoo because they do cool monkey things. Let's make faces at the monkey and see if we can make him throw poo. Perhaps the tall tales and ghost shows are red herrings designed to make us look for imaginary spirits and thus divert attention from an actual spirit who might not want to play ghost games or do ghost tricks.

From the minute I walked into the mansion, I sensed nothing that would give me cause to believe the place was actively haunted. I will use the term "plausibly haunted." The ambiance was warm and inviting and the staff was professional, friendly, and accommodating. There were no neck hairs standing up and no feelings of being watched. It seemed like a beautiful, charming, historical old mansion.

I thought our guide was knowledgeable and credible. Having a very sensitive BS detector, I usually know when the line crosses from fact to fiction. Although our guide admitted to being an actress, I sensed she believed every word she was telling us.

Her dowsing rod session seemed credible and I do believe she was in contact with a spirit of some description. She claims it was Billy, but the spirit seemed subordinate to her and didn't seem like the strong, stern business mogul shown in the photographs.

This spirit, or whatever was moving the dowsing rods to answer questions, seemed timid and obedient. Based on the photographs of Billy, with the hard eyes and staunch demeanor, I would expect someone of Billy's presence not to play so obediently.

Having said that, it is not hard to imagine how a man's spirit might be broken by watching his livelihood destroyed by the very government created to protect his freedoms, not destroy them. I can understand Billy's anger and angst with Prohibition, especially considering the growing police state we have today. If Billy is spinning in his grave, one cannot blame him. I may do the same some day and hope that people don't summon my presence to try to make me do cool ghost tricks. "Hey, Bob, can you use this Ouija board to give us your opinion on the Fourth Amendment?" Me: "Does the term 'rest in peace' mean anything to you?" I digress.

At one point in the dowsing session, "Billy" seemed to be uncomfortable with some spirit in the house.

Our guide said that perhaps a spirit guide that accompanies one of the guests was making him uncomfortable.

She said that "Billy" was communicating to her a picture of an old airplane propeller and something about it was subduing him.

As a pilot with a strong personality, I hoped it wasn't me.

If You Decide to Visit

Location & Contact Info

3322 DeMenil Place

St. Louis, Missouri 63118

Tel: 314-664-8024

E-mail: *patty@lempmansion.com*

Website: *http://www.lempmansion.com/*

Type of Tours & Hunts Offered

The Lemp Experience (ghost hunting packages on select nights); Haunted History Tours on Monday evenings; Comedy-Mystery Dinners on Friday and Saturday nights.

Size: There are 6 suites for rent and 3 stories you can access. The basement (kitchen area) is off limits. No tunnel access.

Price: Starting at $180.00 per night for Sunday–Thursday; Starting at $235.00 per night for Friday and Saturday

Tips & Suggested Itinerary

St. Louis is home to the Gateway Arch. One of the most beautiful parts of the city is the Forest Park area.

The park is composed of 1300 acres and is home to the Saint Louis Art Museum and the Saint Louis Zoo.

The World's Fair Pavilion from 1904 still stands in the park. There are biking and walking trails.

Closest Airports

Lambert-St. Louis International Airport (STL)—about 15 miles away

NINE

The Stanley Hotel
Estes Park, CO

History

The story begins with a man who was running for his life. Freelan Oscar (F.O.) Stanley was a Maine entrepreneur and inventor. Along with his twin brother, Francis, the pair made their first fortune from a photographic process in the late 1800s that they would go on to sell to George Eastman, who later created Kodak. Their second fortune was made by the invention of the Stanley Steamer automobile. Despite his vast wealth, no sum of money could buy F.O.'s way out of the death sentence he was given in 1903. He contracted tuberculosis, and his physician gave him one year to live. It was recommended that he seek Denver's dry climate. When F.O. and his wife Flora arrived in Denver, they quickly realized that the mining town with all the dust and chemicals in the air was not going to help his condition. They made their way to Estes Park, where F.O. stopped running.

The exterior of the Stanley Hotel.

F.O.'s health thrived in Estes Park, and they had a summer home built within the year. (The home is privately owned today.) The couple soon realized that their home was not large enough to host all of their illustrious guests. F.O. began construction on what we know today as the Stanley Hotel. He modeled it in the Georgian Colonial Revival style that was used in their private home.

The Stanley Hotel officially received its first guests on June 22, 1909. Guests would typically stay for an entire summer (June–September), or at least for one entire month. Children, nannies, and other staff were regulated to the fourth floor, where they could sleep and play out of sight of their parents (and without causing any disturbances to the adult guests). Today, the fourth floor is the area of the hotel that seems to be associated with the most ghost stories. It is very common for guests to report that they have heard children running in the hallways or that they have heard the sounds of footsteps on the roof above them. The Stanleys both lived a long—and happy, by many accounts—life, and they used their summer home until F.O. suffered a heart attack and died in 1940. Flora suffered a stroke in the lobby and died at their home in Estes Park a year earlier. Both lived to the age of ninety-one.

The hotel passed through a series of owners after F.O. Stanley and even survived a bankruptcy. In 1974 Stephen King and his wife Tabitha checked in to the hotel during its last open weekend of the season. Back then, the hotel did not have heat and closed for the winter. More about the Stephen King connection later, but suffice it to say for now that this was the fateful night that resulted in *The Shining*.

Stephen King has been very vocal over the years about director Stanley Kubrick's movie adaptation not staying true to his novel. The movie was not filmed at the Stanley Hotel. Instead, Kubrick chose to use exterior and aerial shots of the Timberline Lodge in Oregon (mostly because he desired a higher volume of snow). However, in 1995, Mr. King directed and filmed a three-part miniseries of *The Shining* for ABC that was done at the Stanley Hotel. The current owner, John Cullen, purchased the hotel in 1995 and is said to have been the first owner to ever realize a profit from the hotel. In 2014 the hotel decided to build a version of the hedge maze that Kubrick envisioned for his movie adaptation of King's novel. It was beginning to grow on the front lawn at the time of our visit.

Visiting the Stanley Hotel

I have stayed at the Stanley Hotel a handful of times in the summer over the past eight years. This time was different, though. This time I would stay at the hotel, the same hotel that inspired Stephen King to pen *The Shining*, on Halloween weekend. Bob and I booked a "Ghost Adventure" package. With this package, you get a guaranteed fourth-floor room, your own K-II meter, squishy, glow-in-the-dark Stanley Hotel logo ghost figures, and souvenir "Redrum" mugs.

The lobby of the Stanley.

The original room keys of the hotel are displayed behind the registration desk.

This was Bob's first visit to the Stanley Hotel, so I made sure to point out all of the features of the lobby and the rooms off of the lobby. One of my favorite spots on the property is on a wicker loveseat on the front patio. From here, you can enjoy sweeping views of the Rocky Mountains and check out the antique sleigh on display. An authentic 1906 Stanley Steamer car is on display in the main lobby. According to our guide, it still runs.

The hotel has long since switched to key cards, but I love the nostalgia of the keys on display behind the registration desk. I knew from taking a tour several years ago that the dark wood (faux bois) seen on the lobby walls was a change that was made in 1995 during the filming of *The Shining* miniseries, and I knowingly pointed that out to Bob. Additionally, the "hall of owners" is missing one portrait—that of current owner, John Cullen.

The 1909 brass Otis Elevator has been known to move of its own accord, but it only came when we called it.

Portraits of the Stanley's past owners are displayed in this grand stairway.

*The brass Otis elevator from 1909 still shuttles
the guests to different floors of the hotel.*

We arrived at room 424, where we would spend Halloween night and the night after. While I had stayed here many times in the past, I had never booked a session with Madame Vera, the Stanley's resident psychic.

I got on the phone and booked our readings before I unpacked a single suitcase. Madame Vera was a pleasure to meet, and we highly recommend that you include a reading with her on your itinerary. I am not including specific details about our readings for privacy reasons.

After our readings, I decided to change my reservation for the nightly ghost tour to a day tour. Bob had injured his leg and would not be able to walk the stairs of all four floors of the hotel. I would attend the tour alone, and I anticipated that Halloween night would be a little too crowded for my introvert's tastes.

Tours are open to guests of the hotel as well as to the public. The Stanley Tour Office is on the ground floor of the hotel.

The mirrored bar in the Piñon Room.

The path of our tour began in the Piñon and Billiard Rooms before we made our way next door to the Music Room; through the lobby to learn a bit about the Stanley Steamer; into the MacGregor Room; up the main staircase, stopping briefly outside of room 217; up the former servants' side stairs, stopping outside of room 401; and finally to the basement tunnel room.

Piñon and Billiard Rooms

These rooms were built for the men of the day to relax and play indoors. You can practically still hear the sounds of the clanking ivory pool balls and smell the cigar smoke. Contrary to the lobby, the dark wood paneling in this room is authentic. There is an original mirrored bar that remains inside the Piñon Room. This is the bar that is shown in Stephen King's miniseries version of *The Shining*.

The ladies were allowed in the Billiard Room, but only if they sat on the bench as spectators.

The beautiful wooden bench in the Billiard Room.

If you are sitting on the bench today and look to your left, you will see what is now the Chrysalis Gift Shop. In F.O. and Flora's time, this room was a Ladies' Writing Room.

The Music Room and Flora Stanley

In *Stanley Ghost Stories*, there is a very interesting photo that appears to be the ghostly image of Flora Stanley. The Music Room was said to be her favorite room, after all. The Steinway grand piano is off-limits, yet guests call down to the front desk at all hours of the night to complain of the sounds that are emitting from the piano. Flora was particularly fond of Strauss. Staff members will go check the Music Room to make sure no one has succeeded in sneaking in. Their search results will inevitably turn up an empty room. F.O. gifted the piano to Flora during the opening weekend in 1909. John Philip Sousa was said to have personally tuned and played this piano in the early 1930s.

The Music Room of the Stanley hotel.

Witnesses have reported seeing the apparition of Flora Stanley right before them and smelling the strong scent of roses when there were none in the room. This room has retained its original white plaster interior. It is affectionately called the "wedding cake" room by many brides who have booked their celebrations here.

Whiskey Bar and Cascades Restaurant

Fans of Jim Carrey and the movie *Dumb and Dumber* might recognize this area from the movie. Paranormal buffs will be interested to discover that the tabletops are made of hammered copper, which is a material thought to be a natural conductor for energy.

The MacGregor Room

This was and still is a formal dining room. In 1911 an explosion occurred in room 217, which is directly above this room. Elizabeth Wilson was a housekeeper who was injured while attempting to light a gas lamp. The explosion caused her to fall from room 217 down to the floor of this dining room.

Room 217—Elizabeth Wilson and the Stephen King Connection

As mentioned above, Elizabeth Wilson was a loyal employee who was injured while attempting to light a gas lamp. Apparently there was a leak, and when she went to light the lamp, it caused an explosion that destroyed approximately 10 percent of the hotel. Mr. Stanley very generously paid all of her medical bills, and she healed and eventually returned to her post. Our tour guide told us that she continued to work until she died (eighty-some years of age). Common reports are made by guests to the hotel staff that they continue to receive Mrs. Wilson's world-class service of unpacking their suitcases and tucking them in at night. Sometimes guests believe that Mrs. Wilson is expressing her disapproval of unmarried couples staying in the room by playing tricks on them. One couple even wrote in the guest book that they felt like an invisible (yet physical) barrier was between them in the middle of their bed. That type of thing was not supposed to happen in her time, so modern guests might find her spirit to be just a tad judgmental.

It was the last open weekend of the season in 1974 when a young writer by the name of Stephen King checked in to the hotel with his wife. They would be the only guests for the night. Mr. King had already published *Carrie* and had finished *Salem's Lot*. According to George Beahm's 1992 book, *The Stephen King Story: A Literary Profile*, the author had moved his family to Boulder to work on a setting for a new story. He was tinkering around with the idea of a little boy who had psychic abilities. The setting was tentatively inside a haunted amusement park, but he was stuck. That was as far as he got with the idea—until the author and his wife dined alone in the hotel's restaurant, and Tabitha went to bed in the best room in the house—room 217. Mr. King was left to his own devices, and he did a walkabout through the halls of the abandoned hotel.

I have not been able to find any account that details whether or not he believed he had a personal paranormal experience during his walkabout. Whatever happened to him on their night alone in the hotel, though, inspired him to write *The Shining*. We do not know if Mrs. Wilson came to call on the Kings in 1974, but there was a claw-foot bathtub in the room they stayed in, which no doubt played a role in inspiring that famous scene concerning Mrs. Massey. Beahm wrote about King's stay, "He imagined the fire hoses coming alive, thumping across the carpet. 'By then,' King recalled, 'whatever it is that makes you want to make things up ... was turned on. I was scared, but I loved it.'" King has said that he was glad when he was finished writing the tub scene. Further, on Steven King's online library, the author has posted the story of his inspiration for the novel. He said he thought the hotel was the perfect setting for a ghost story, and he dreamed that his son was being chased by a fire hose. When he woke from the dream, he lit a cigarette and sat at a window that faced the Rocky Mountains. By the time he was finished with his cigarette, he had outlined his novel. Rebecca Pittman quotes King in *The History & Haunting of the Stanley Hotel*. When discussing the inspiration behind the novel, he reportedly said: "It was like God had put me there to hear that and see those things." King is never more specific, and he just refers to the "atmosphere" of the hotel.

Vortex Stairs

The staircase area just outside room 217 is known by many psychics and sensitives as being a vortex portal area, where it is believed that many spirits travel. Some might have been former hotel guests or employees, and some might have never stayed at the hotel during their lifetime. If you tilt your head back and look up to the top floor, you just might find yourself experiencing a dizzy spell.

Room 401

Lord Dunraven gets blamed for much of what guests experience while staying in this room. He was a real character in the late 1800s in Estes Park, but he does not have a real connection to the hotel. The closest connection I could find was that F.O. bought the land from Dunraven and wanted to name the hotel after him, but the locals rallied and signed a petition to name the hotel after F.O. instead. Dunraven's portrait hangs in the hotel and women have claimed to see him in this room. According to many storytellers, Lord Dunraven was a notorious womanizer, so maybe the former room of nannies and housekeepers is the perfect place for his spirit to knock about. Room 401 was famously portrayed in an episode of *Ghost Hunters*, where viewers watched evidence of a closet door opening and closing on its own (and then appearing to latch by itself), as well as a glass on a nightstand table that appeared to spontaneously combust.

My guide told us that the front desk receives five to six calls per week about happenings in this room, and approximately six calls every year specifically related to lost wedding rings. I have to tell you, if you stay in this room, sleep with your ring on!

The Endless Hallway

The "endless hallway" begins right outside room 424, where we stayed. The length of the hallway appears to be considerably longer than the hallway on the other wing of the fourth floor. It is not hard to imagine the effect that this hallway could have (or did have) on Stephen King when he wrote about those young female twins first appearing in *The Shining*. There is a little nook area in this hallway where two small loveseats are stationed. Remember, this area of the hotel used to be essentially an indoor playground for the children of the esteemed guests. Ghost hunters like to try experiments here by leaving candy out to see if it will spark any paranormal activity.

The legendary endless hallway.

The stairs to the Tower.

The entrance to the employee tunnel.

Stairs to the Tower

Stop and look at the barrier that separates the hotel from the roof. "Red rum" was written here several years ago by an unknown guest. In the early days of the hotel, the children were allowed access to play on the roof. This was no doubt a very heavy-traffic area.

The Tunnel

Perhaps what is so intriguing about this area of the hotel is that you can see for yourself that it's built into the quartz mountain. The Stanley does not have a dark history or a lot of deaths that might commonly fuel a lot of paranormal stories. This was a summer place, and it was by all accounts a happy place. It feels like a joyful place to me, still. The tunnel was originally built in the early 1980s as a means for employees to travel from their dormitories at the back of the property into the hotel without exposing themselves to the harsh winter elements. You can see huge tree trunks coming out of the rocks. Paranormal investigators routinely submit evidence of EVPs and interesting photos from this area of the hotel.

In 2014's *America's Most Haunted*, Theresa Argie and her coauthor, Eric Olsen, reported on a documentary called *The Stanley Effect: A Piezoelectric Nightmare*. The end theory can be summarized as attributing the hauntings to the geology of the minerals found in the mountain and the addition of a nearby power plant. Argie and Olsen go on to explain, "Properties in the environment can act as a sort of amplifier of paranormal activity. Crystals are thought to direct, absorb, and multiply energy, and the mountain is full of crystals." The Stanley is primely positioned in a natural environment that very well could be amplifying the residual and intelligent hauntings that so many people have been reporting at this site for years. We find ourselves circling back to the stone tape theory that we have discussed in earlier chapters of this book. The crystals and quartz have possibly taped energy from the past and are playing and releasing this energy on occasion, resulting in the hauntings. Argie and Olsen also point out that the hotel is considered a "free-floating building," and that it moves with the mountain.

Sleeping at the Stanley Hotel

It was Halloween night at the Stanley Hotel and we decided to relax by enjoying a viewing of *The Shining*. It definitely helped set the scene. The Shining Masquerade Ball was in full effect down at the Concert Hall. While the hallways and lobby areas were not packed to the gills by any means, it was still not going to be a quiet night to walk the property, so I opted for a 6:00 a.m. call the following morning. When I woke the next morning, I found that the glasses I had stored on the nightstand were mysteriously inside my closed suitcase. I do not believe I did it while sleeping, and Bob swore that he didn't do it. I would be quick to dismiss this entire incident if I hadn't had something similar occur in room

418 during a summer visit in 2010. During that stay, I woke to find my camera missing, and when we found it, it was posed directly under the middle of the bed. For some reason, my things seem to move around when I stay at the Stanley Hotel in a way they don't when I'm at home or staying in other hotels.

My own personal walkabout in the early morning hours of November 1 was essentially uneventful. Nothing jumped out at me and screamed "boo!" while I sat alone on the bench in the billiards room. I walked the entire property but for whatever reason, I was not able to tap into any energy lingering around the hotel. I am not a medium, so I have no gift that allows me to see spirits. One of the things that I have found frustrating as an author and as a paranormal traveler is that some of the members of the public seem to think that when they are entering a famously "haunted" public place, they are somehow purchasing a ticket to a guaranteed 1-800-Ghosts-On-Demand free-for-all fright night. I would like to educate people that life does not work like that. There is no switch flipped at midnight that lets the ghosts out, to roam in the hallways of the fourth floor. We are talking about real human spirits. There is no controlling what happens, when it happens, or if anything *will* happen. Sometimes I am followed by something that shows up on a tape recorder saying, "Jamie, they want Jamie." Other times, I walk the hallways, seemingly alone. Or do I? I ask that question because the day was brand new, and the hotel was not finished with me yet. Nobody came when I called, but something decided to come when I wasn't asking for it to come.

That night, I took a shower and was in the bathroom drying my hair. I had my head tipped forward with my hair spilling upside down. Suddenly, out of the corner of my eye, I saw something walk past the door. What's the problem, you ask? Nobody else was in the room. Bob had gone to make a run to the pharmacy down the hill.

I sat frozen in place on the lid of the closed commode and waited for my husband to get back so I could walk from the bathroom to the bed. Maybe F.O. stopped running when he found Estes Park, but for me, there is no stopping for long when it comes to the Stanley Hotel.

Comments from Bob

The Stanley Hotel is rich in tradition and has a well-documented haunted history. We arrived on Halloween and walked into a full-blown festival with adults dressed in their Halloween best. As we pulled our suitcases into the lobby, we walked past a zombie with bloodstains on her chest and a knife sticking out of her neck. Her date was a dead ringer for Freddie Krueger. It was like an NFL Sunday for the Halloween enthusiast.

I tried to overcome my natural caution with the paranormal on this trip, but my caution remained. Having serious concerns about the wisdom of interacting with things of an unknown nature, which can see and affect me when I cannot see them, I decided I would be safer as an observer rather than a participant. I figured I could sneak under the radar if I didn't engage with them. Maybe they would leave me alone, especially since there were hundreds of others who were, either wittingly or unwittingly, actively engaging with them.

Our session with Madame Vera was genuine and entirely credible. Her words resonated with my spirit. Over the next two days, Jamie and I walked through and around the halls and grounds of the hotel and the warmness of the people and the history were very enjoyable. The beauty of the hotel grounds and the surrounding area were beyond words. The Stanley Hotel was charming and warm, its staff and customers cordial and polite. Like Jamie, I cannot say that the haunted energy lingering in the hotel jumped out and grabbed me, which suited me just fine. I didn't want anything messing with me and nothing did.

With regard to Jamie's thoughts about not being able to flip a switch and let the ghosts out, I agree 100 percent. As it pertains to paranormal activity, absence of evidence is not evidence of absence. If there was a way for the paranormal to be manipulated by flipping a switch, metaphysical theories could more easily be developed. Instead, it is hit or miss. Places seem active and electric at times, warm and embracing in other times, angry and agitated in certain instances, or completely silent in others. But as strong as the spiritual essence of a place can be, it seems to run in the background as the movement, noise, and human energy of normal day to day events overshadow the spirit world, at least for the most part. I strongly believe the condition of our own spirit dictates the level to which we can be affected. At least that's what I tell myself. That allows things unseen to remain in nice little boxes in my mind. It works well until one wakes up and finds one's camera under the bed, and eyeglasses packed inside a suitcase.

If You Decide to Visit

Location & Contact Info

333 Wonderview Avenue

Estes Park, Colorado 80517

Tel: 1-800-976-1377

E-mail: info@stanleyhotel.com

Website: *http://www.stanleyhotel.com/*

Type of Tours & Hunts Offered

The Stanley day tour is a 90 minute tour that is conducted between 10:00 a.m. and 5:00 p.m. Adults who are hotel guests pay $20.00; Children 12 & under pay $17.00. Ghost tours run at night, beginning at 6:00 p.m. Adults who are hotel guests pay $25.00. There are no prices listed for children for the ghost tours, but the age limit is listed as 10+. Ghost stories are offered for families. The hotel offers 5 hour paranormal investigations to those who are 18 years of age and older. Guests of the hotel can book the investigation for $55.00 per person.

Size: 4 floors in the main hotel; approximately 40 rooms in The Lodge (formerly known as The Manor House); luxury condos are behind the property.

Price: weekly rates start at $299.00 per night (summer 2016)

Tips & Suggested Itinerary

Explore the village of Estes Park and hike the Rocky Mountains.

Closest Airports

Denver International Airport (DEN)—about 75 miles away

Cheyenne Regional Airport (CYS)—about 89 miles away

TEN

The Palmer House Hotel
Sauk Centre, MN

Sauk Centre, Minnesota—the hometown city that once inspired Sinclair Lewis to write a novel called *Main Street*. Sinclair Lewis was the first American to win the Nobel Prize in Literature in 1930. Four years earlier, he famously declined the Pulitzer for his 1926 novel, *Arrowsmith*. The reasons he reportedly gave are quoted on the Sinclair Lewis Society website. Essentially, he did not agree with an arbitrary committee selecting one best novel of the year to embody the popular code of whatever they interpreted as the "wholesome atmosphere of American life" (FAQ). His debut novel, *Main Street*, was published in 1920 and was, in simplest terms, a novel about the banality of small-town life in Sauk Centre, Minnesota (referred to as Gopher Prairie in the book). The book was an instant best seller, although it wasn't exactly popular with the locals, since it was a satire about the narrow-mindedness of small-town middle-class Americans. The main character, Carol, is in her midtwenties when she marries one of the town's doctors and moves from St. Paul to Gopher Prairie. She has big plans to bring culture to the town, but she is not well received.

Sinclair Lewis worked as a night desk clerk in the Palmer House Hotel (which he referred to as the Minniemashie House in *Main Street* and the American House in *Work of Art*) briefly during the summer of 1902. He was even reported to have lived on-site at the Palmer House in one of the upstairs sleeping rooms. The legend is that he was fired on multiple occasions for writing and reading instead of doing his job. His descriptions of the Minniemashie House throughout *Main Street* are not exactly flattering. I do not know if he took creative license with that or if he was writing from his true perspective of working there in the early 1900s.

Like his character, Carol, Lewis did make it out of Sauk Centre. When Carol made it out, her freedom had an emptiness to it. There was no contentment with anything or any place. It matters not what the change is, as soon as the change becomes routine (and it always will), the dull emptiness of life starts to set in, and then you are running again. I suspect that Sinclair found the same thing to be true in his own life. He made it all the way to international celebrity status and maintained a life of extensive travel, because to stay in one place too long killed his writing ability and ambition. He was a restless soul who never really made a home anywhere. He died a lonely alcoholic in Italy in 1951. Whatever he was looking for, I suspect he never found it in life. Though many believe he is still searching for something in the afterlife, continually popping into the Palmer House.

Today, the Palmer House Hotel retains its charm, and it looks to me like a great example of authentic old America—essentially a perfect example of a place that has fought and won against the big corporate chains and big-brother government trying to kill it. Long may she reign. Main Street is still there, too.

The exterior of the Palmer House Hotel.

The main street of Sauk Centre, Minnesota.

History

In the late 1800s, the Sauk Centre House was the first hotel in town, and it occupied the same corner on Main Street as the Palmer House does now. A fire on June 26, 1900, destroyed the Sauk Centre House, and Ralph and Christina Palmer built the Palmer House in 1901. According to the hotel's website, there were originally thirty-eight rooms with a common bathroom shared by guests on each floor. In 1993 the hotel was remodeled and there are now nineteen rooms, all with private bathrooms. Many of the original architectural features have been maintained and preserved over the years, and the hotel is listed as a National Historic Site. In the lobby, you can still see the original tin ceilings, although they have been painted over by a previous owner. There are Venetian stained-glass windows throughout the lobby, and a grand main staircase remains.

The Legends

One of the former owners, Al Tingley, wrote a book about his experience living, working, and owning the hotel.

The lobby of the Palmer House Hotel features stained-glass windows.

Original fixtures are located throughout the Palmer House Hotel.

The book is called *Corner on Main Street* and was published in 1984. It is an entertaining read about modern life and owning a small business in small-town America. Toward the end of the book, Tingley discloses that they've discovered a ghost (or ghosts). This was a big deal, because in those days it wasn't popular to talk about such things. In fact, they were afraid that it would hurt the business, so they tried to keep a lid on it. Still, there were footsteps heard where no humans were walking. Employees and guests alike had experiences that they could not explain away. Rooms could become chillingly cold with no discernible reason. Once a maid was even locked inside room 13. Tingley himself has written that he heard the unexplainable sounds of children's voices and giggling.

As far as deaths at the Palmer House, Tingley wrote that he discovered that there was a suicide in the hotel upstairs somewhere, and a man reportedly hung himself in the bar by jumping from the pool table.

The staircase at the Palmer House Hotel.

During Tingley's ownership, they also had an elderly gentleman die of natural causes while sitting on a chair in the lobby. Even back then, Tingley and his friends and associates talked among themselves about the possibility of the spirit of Sinclair Lewis still popping in from time to time. In January 1951, an urn containing the ashes of Sinclair Lewis was brought to Sauk Centre from Rome.

Tingley wrote about his memory of that day and of Dr. Claude Lewis, Sinclair's brother, emptying the ashes and then watching as they were scattered and carried by a light breeze. Many years later, while in the hotel, he would experience another light breeze that would recall that memory to his mind.

In Michael Norman's *The Nearly Departed: Minnesota Ghost Stories & Legends,* there are tales of full-body apparitions that have interacted with some of the employees. Norman recounts a tale of Kelley Freese and one of her employees comparing notes on the appearance of one man they both saw on separate occasions.

The stranger ordered a beer and paid with quarters one night when the desk clerk was on duty alone (there were no registered guests that evening). When she described him to Kelley, Kelley remembered that a few days earlier she saw what sounded like the same man in the description walk past her in the hallway.

An apparition of a ghost boy has been seen on the main staircase as well as throughout the hotel. Disembodied faces have been seen in the basement. Books have flown off the shelves.

The most fascinating modern legend is of course that of the spirit of Sinclair Lewis himself, who is believed to interact with many guests, employees, and the owner herself. Recently, paranormal television shows have featured the Palmer House Hotel and have explored the idea that Sinclair Lewis hid a lost novel somewhere within the hotel. It is mind-boggling to even consider. The lost great American novel? Wow!

The basement stairs of the Palmer House Hotel.

Our Stay

We arrived at the house around 4:00 p.m. At this time of day, the light coming through the stained-glass windows in the lobby is very subdued, calming, and has the effect of transporting you back in time. I admired the black and white photographs that were on display as well as a cabinet containing some exhibits dedicated to Sinclair Lewis. We were given the key to room 6 on the second floor and rested awhile before our tour would begin around 5:00 p.m. There must be some kind of power with the afternoon light, the green paint, and how it all mixes together to make my mood. I remember thinking, "This is a special place." I asked Bob if he had a sense of anything, and he said the first thing that naturally came to his mind: "Plausibly haunted." For the superstitious among you, the hotel is said to be built on the main crossroads of the town.

Kelley Freese, the owner of the Palmer House Hotel, met a small group of us downstairs in the restaurant to begin our tour. She is authentic, hospitable, and one of the most down-to-earth people I have ever met.

There were a few things that she did in particular that made me reach this conclusion about authenticity. The first thing that she did that struck a high note with me was that she sat on the counter in the restaurant and faced all of us, introduced herself, and opened herself up to a completely random Q&A session, where she entertained questions from everyone who had something to ask. This ranged from paranormal stories to sharing her experiences with the *Ghost Adventures* crew (all reported to us as positive experiences). Prior to my visit, I saw both episodes of the *Ghost Adventures* show that covered the Palmer House Hotel, including the "Aftershocks" episode, so I was of course very curious about the Sinclair Lewis connection. Kelley was completely forthright in answering all of my questions about that, and she said that yes, there was about a thirty-minute EVP session where it seemed like they were communicating with the spirit of Sinclair Lewis and that he was leading them to an area of the house where his lost papers are. To date, she has not started tearing into the structure of the hotel itself looking for the missing manuscript. (And you, Dear Reader, better respect her hotel and refrain from checking in with a sledgehammer.) She does maintain that she believes she was led to the house for a reason, and that it is something that goes back to her childhood. She believes there is an end story, but just isn't sure yet what that ending will be, exactly.

There has also been plenty of media coverage concerning the mysterious missing box of rib bones from underneath the basement stairs. A 2012 article titled "Is Palmer House Hotel in Sauk Centre Haunted?" which ran in the Saint Paul *Pioneer Press*, reported that "after a stranger told her about a dream that directed her to the spot, Freese says she dug up what looked like rib bones in the basement.

She put them in a box, but when she returned for them, the box had—you guessed it—disappeared." In my opinion, the weird part is not at all that they found rib bones, but that they disappeared. Mr. Palmer kept dogs in kennels very close to these stairs, so it would seem plausible to me that they just found historic leftovers that Mr. Palmer had fed to his dogs!

Kelley briefed us about the background of the hotel—there was a brief time when there was a flu epidemic in town, and the Palmer House served as an overflow hospital. It is very possible that the basement served as a morgue as well. She also shared her own personal story about coming to own the building. When she and her husband purchased the hotel in 2002, it was to save the building. They had no idea of any haunted history tied to the Palmer House. Somehow, during the group's Q&A session, the subject of crossing spirits came up. Kelley said that she has let people who seemed reputable or professional assist in crossing some of the spirits that have made contact in the Palmer House. When I heard that, I noted it to mention in the book because not all property owners feel that way. Some people have flat-out told us that they have a "no crossing" policy. It would appear that some owners are not open to helping spirits find peace, and that they wish to trap them in the building (if at all possible). Kelley is the complete opposite of that. She stated that the Palmer House has taught her how to think out of the box, and she enjoys having a safe place where other people can come and think out of the box as well.

Many people were curious and new to the paranormal field, and Kelley answered questions in a way that seemed completely believable and in line with many of my own personal experiences and beliefs. We talked as a group about the possibility of travelers coming back and forth as well as some "permanent non-registered guests or residents." One theory about all of the hauntings could be in line with what is going on at the famous Stanley Hotel in Estes Park, Colorado. The paranormal theory with some of the hotels featured in this book isn't the same as some of the theories I discussed in my first book, *Haunted Asylums, Prisons, and Sanatoriums*, in the sense that so many people died on site that spirits are trapped there. In contrast, some of these hotels are places that were so happy and wonderful while people were alive that many seem to be coming back and checking in again for a while! Even though it has always technically been a hotel, Kelley pointed out to us that in its earlier history, there were tenants at the Palmer House, not just guests who stayed briefly for a visit. The fact that the Palmer House was home to countless people and families has to have some kind of residual pull. While rooms 11 and 17 seem to be written about the most as being haunted, Kelley pointed out that activity can happen anywhere throughout the hotel, and at any time.

Interestingly, Kelley told us that the Palmer House was the first hotel west of the Twin Cities to have electricity. One of the most common occurrences in the hotel is for lights to flash on and off by themselves. Kelley commented that when the first group of guests came once the electricity was installed, they blew out the lights playing with the switches! She floated the idea of the spirits still being amused by this modern "novelty." That certainly seems plausible to me. I do believe in the possibility of places simply being naturally charged or haunted. I do think that there are some places where the veil is just a little bit thinner. This could be one of those places.

Lastly, the third most authentic detail about my experience was that Kelley refrained from telling us any scary stories before she led us down into the basement to begin our mini ghost-hunting session.

Down in the basement

Our small group followed two female volunteers and Kelley into the basement. It was well lit until we settled into chairs, which were arranged in a circle in one of the rooms. Oddly enough, the group was composed of a few preteen girls and their mothers, a few girls in their early twenties, and me and Bob. He was the only male, and I thought how cool it was to have such a large group of almost all females interested in the paranormal. The lights were turned off, and Kelley's K-II meter sat on the floor in the center of our circle. Kelley began the session, but everyone had an opportunity to speak if they wanted. It was blacker than black down there, and it took a long time (probably thirty minutes) for my eyes to even begin discerning the pipes above my head. There were times when it seemed that the darkness was getting darker, if that makes sense. I couldn't see the faces of the people sitting right next to me the entire time we were down there. We all stated our intention as far as whether or not we were open to getting touched. Bob and I were the only ones who declined to give permission. Later, once back at home, I read Adrian Lee's chapter about the Palmer House in his 2012 book, *Mysterious Minnesota*. Mr. Lee sheds some light on the possible increasing darkness we experienced while in the first room of the basement. His theory behind this is that it's caused by a Native American elemental. He describes what is called a "Pukwudgie" on page 41: "This energy made its arrival known to me via the heavy smell of sulfur and the act of engulfing investigators in blackness—so they completely disappear on a night vision camera (as if a dark blanket has been thrown over them); dog-like snuffling and growling noises have also been recorded on my equipment."

There were two girls who volunteered to sit near the door to watch for shadows. Some people thought they saw things—mists, shadows, firefly-looking lights. Bob and I did not observe or experience anything in this first room except for at the very end of the session. One of the guests started asking questions related to the use of the K-II meter, and it randomly shot all the way up to red, as if it was answering her question. That was unexplainable and downright weird. The thing about talking to spirits in a group such as this is that sometimes not everyone understands that we are not entering an amusement park ride and that there are no guarantees of anything happening. Sometimes you sit in the dark and nothing really happens. Everyone with us that evening seemed to understand that concept.

We moved on to the next room in the basement, and I became a little bit more vocal and started asking about Sinclair Lewis. Someone added in that if anyone could hear us that knew where Sinclair was, if they could go get him and bring him down, we would appreciate it. We all continued our turns talking, and some more people thought they saw shadow activity outside the door. A few minutes later, an extreme cold feeling suddenly entered the room. This was not the air conditioning kicking in or a breeze coming through an open window. This was a cold that I have read about, heard about, and even seen portrayed on television and in the movies. It came out of nowhere and seemed to have a thickness to it. Someone said, "Maybe they just brought Sinclair down."

If this was so, this was likely my best opportunity to talk to him. I told the man I was reading his book (*Main Street*) and planned to finish it tonight upstairs in our room. I did not tell him that I was struggling with finishing it because it was so long and that I knew all about his mentor, Upton Sinclair, pretty much telling him the exact same thing. I thought it, though, and if he could read my mind, I was busted. We cannot know who or what (if anyone) was down there in the basement with us that night, but I can tell you that I believe something was going on that cannot be simply explained away.

But Why Would Sinclair Lewis Haunt a Building Where He Just Briefly Worked?

In an attempt to answer this question and to learn more about the man behind the celebrity, I read Richard Lingeman's 2002 biography entitled *Sinclair Lewis: Rebel From Main Street.* One of the major themes of Sinclair Lewis's life was rootlessness, loneliness, and disconnectedness. When Sinclair Lewis (also known as "Red") was first out of Yale, he worked as a journalist in an office and it drove him mad to be cooped up in one place for endless hours at a time. He was a good worker, but he just always wanted to be somewhere else. He became obsessed with freedom and travel, and the day he was finally able to quit his day job as a newspaperman, he yelled, "I'm a free man. I've escaped from bondage. I told Doran what I thought of him today and I'm out" (Lingeman). He felt that travel was the only mechanism that helped him gather material for his books. So he kept moving. He made about three million dollars from *Main Street*, and that bought his freedom from ever having to participate in the mundane office life again. The other side of that was he felt the literati/aristocracy class looked down on him like a trained monkey. He didn't fit anywhere anymore, so he made his life's work his new religion and began his slow descent into alcoholism.

The result was that he would effectively remove himself from the world so that he was too far gone to ever come back. He tried, though. *Work of Art* featured some of his memories growing up around the Palmer House and was considered by Lewis himself as his "most serious novel." After twenty years, he finally began to desire settling down, and he began *The Quiet Mind*, which Lingeman says to have been inspired by his readings of Thoreau "and the importance of one's roots." He rented a house on Lake Minnetonka in March of 1942 and declared his love for the great state of Minnesota once more. But, like everything else, it was not to last for long. Lewis found that try as he might, he could not go home again. In fact, the character of Lloyd McGarg in Thomas Wolfe's 1940 novel *You Can't Go Home Again* was modeled after Lewis himself! The spell that Minnesota once cast on him was broken. He returned to New York in September and continued to roll like a stone until his death of a massive heart attack in Rome on January 10, 1951.

Given what we know about how he struggled with always looking for a home, it is very plausible that he is still struggling with this very thing in death. He had a lot of success, but the man himself was plagued with a series of problems that kept him from ever finding peace and happiness while he was alive. Maybe he isn't lost and searching anymore, after all. Maybe, just maybe, after all this time, he has finally succeeded and found himself back home.

If you make it to the Palmer House Hotel and you find yourself sitting alone in the darkness of the basement, give old Red my regards. We are all just travelers in our individual stages of trying to find our way back home.

Comments from Bob

The visit to the Palmer House was an experience that shaped my views. As I mentioned, I came into this venture as a neophyte with no real theories about the paranormal but numerous experiences in my life that I attributed to that realm. I have always sensed there was something to the topic but came into this venture with an open mind and heart. I am not trying to prove a point or influence the reader in any way.

Kelley, the owner of the Palmer House Hotel, had a very healthy and down-to-earth view about the topic of ghosts, and while they are much like my own, her way of explaining opened my eyes considerably. She is a very good speaker and a genuinely good human being with her heart very much in the right place. Like Jamie and me, Kelley believes we are dealing with human souls, and these deserve to be treated with dignity, respect, and mercy.

Many of the spirits in the Palmer House Hotel, according to Kelley, are transient in nature. Some are earthbound spirits, while others have crossed over into the light and choose to pop in from time to time. All have different stories.

Her story about the earthbound spirit who was afraid to cross over into the light in fear of eternal damnation touched me deeply. According to Kelley, one of her guests made contact with this spirit and realized the spirit was in fear. The spirit had lived in Sauk Centre and her husband had died. Having no money, no income, and two small children to feed, she saw no other option than to sell her body. She became a woman of the night. The elders of the church, not hesitating to throw the first stone, were judgmental and told her she would burn in Hell. (God, save us from your followers!) When she died, the story said she was afraid to go toward the light fearing God's wrath, and she became an earthbound spirit. Eventually, Kelley's guest was able to help this spirit cross over, hopefully to a place of rest and peace.

I can understand the fear of death. If I lived a life of guilt based on my choices and believed that eternal Hell awaited me because of my choices, I might be afraid of the light as well.

Regarding Sinclair Lewis, I believe he was a restless wanderer, dreamer, nonconformist, stubborn realist, rugged individualist, and independent thinker. Had we lived in the same place and time, we would have been friends. We walked many of the same paths. He was also very human, and like many writers, he had a problem with the bottle. I believe he was misunderstood and disillusioned, and he perhaps died in a mental state that might have posed challenges to crossing over.

In the basement when they asked if he was there and if he wanted to communicate, I sensed that he was having trouble focusing enough energy to consistently light up the K-II meter. (I can barely work the thing with my hands.) I can't prove any of this, but I sense his frustration might have been why the room temperature dropped several degrees immediately. If I was in the same room with him, even for an instant, I consider myself honored.

If You Decide to Visit

Location & Contact Info

The Palmer House Hotel

500 Sinclair Lewis Avenue

Sauk Centre, MN 56378

Website: *http://www.thepalmerhousehotel.com/index.html*

Type of Tours & Hunts Offered

Check the hotel's website for a list of paranormal and social events. They routinely offer historic tours and groups can request investigations by filling out a questionnaire for consideration.

Size: 4 Stories—basement for investigations; Lobby and bar/restaurant area on the main floor; Floors 3 and 4 for rooms.

Price: $71.99–$184.99 per night

Tips & Suggested Itinerary

Take in a movie at the charming Main Street Theatre.

The Sinclair Lewis Museum is open Memorial Day through Labor Day and is free. The address is: 1220 Main Street S, Sauk Centre, MN 56378. His boyhood home is located at 810 Sinclair Lewis Avenue and is open for tours in the summer.

Closest Airports

Minneapolis–Saint Paul International Airport (MSP)— about 119 miles away

Hector International Airport (FAR)—about 133 miles away

Conclusion

We have now reached the part of the journey where all that is left to do is reflect back on what happened to us. I did not set out specifically to investigate any particular hotel. All of these places effectively found me through their undeniable reputations as being "haunted." Looking back, though, there were common theories and characteristics about these places that kept coming up. Words and characteristics such as these:

- Located at a crossroads
- Piezoelectric effect
- Stone tape theory
- Former hospitals
- Former mining towns
- Quartz, copper, limestone, and crystal
- Bleed throughs and place memory
- Vortexes with swirling water underground
- Miles of underground tunnels

I did not go into this journey believing strongly beforehand that geology somehow plays such a role in places that we call "haunted." I certainly knew some of the theories, and I believed that it was possible, but now that I have seen and investigated ten more of some of the most commonly "haunted" places in America, I would say that I do strongly believe in geological reasons (or at least possible geological contributing causes) for "hauntings." I am not ready to go so far as saying "the rock made me see a ghost," but I am ready to say something like:"the copper (or other mineral) is a natural conductor and very well could be making the veil just a little bit thinner here." If I rely on what my body feels, I believe that there are places that have some sort of natural magic to them. Maybe I was just standing under a power line that I hadn't noticed, but some places just felt powerfully charged. The strongest natural charge by far was in the town of Eureka Springs. The fact that it was full of limestone and sixty-two natural springs is not a lost coincidence on me.

You might have picked up this book because you are a fan of the paranormal and simply hoped to be entertained. What I write is nonfiction travel reports, and so, like life itself, it is not always "entertaining" in the summer blockbuster sense. I am relating my true paranormal experiences to you. I have never come face-to-face with a rotting corpse in room 237. I never got chased by a monster in a dark basement, or terrorized by an evil doll that chased me around an abandoned mansion on a dark Louisiana voodoo night. But there were real things that happened, nonetheless. Some of them cannot be explained away.

Maybe you picked up this book because you are going through something in your life and are looking for answers. I would give them to you if I could, but my most honest advice would be for you to find truth in yourself and through the interpretation of your own experiences. I have strong feelings about PROOF and TRUTH. These feelings have changed how I see the world.

A Word on "Proof" and "Truth"

I am not a scientist, but I do have a legal background and generally grasp the concept of evidence. Over the years of working on cases and being a trial paralegal, it is hard for me to believe in any earthly or worldly thing absolutely. I would say I am a no bullshit type of person, and when my detector goes off, I listen to it. Nothing is really real to me now except for the way I feel about it. Even that, I know, is not a foolproof system. (I am channeling Charles Dickens's *A Christmas Carol*: "You may be an undigested bit of beef, a blot of mustard, a crumb of cheese, a fragment of underdone potato. There's more of gravy than of grave about you, whatever you are!")

I have lived in a world of madness where there is no such thing as the truth—only two sides arguing vehemently over their version of the facts (and both sides completely convinced that they are the "good guys"). If one side argues better in front of the judge that the truth is too prejudicial, guess what? The jury is not told "the truth."

Thus, that sums up how I feel about proof. We all have our versions and ideas for what truth is. Most of the theories begin with the word "arguably ... xyz." Arguably, the flashlight could have circuited out, for thirty minutes, seemingly in response to my direct line of questioning ... While captured on my iPhone video function. Repeatedly. In many different locations over the years. Arguably, I ate a piece of cheese that caused me to have a nightmare.

We think we are doing something with this equipment we use in order to seek "evidence" that there are such things as spirits or ghosts, but in the end, we really can't know what we are doing, so what is it really worth? Would we be better served to rely on our senses? Probably, but how I feel changes quite frequently. How can there ever be any "proof"? People have very strong opinions about the paranormal. You can view my flashlight videos on YouTube, read my writings, and then go visit the locations for yourself and see what you experience and feel. There is no proof other than what you can hold within your own mind. I do believe that there is something out there in the great beyond that I have communicated with. Whether or not it is a ghost always remains up for debate.

I am not a psychic, your minister, a healer, a medium, a counselor, or your God. I am merely your fellow traveler.

I implore you to go and see.

Bibliography

Argie, Theresa and Eric Olsen. *America's Most Haunted.* New York: Berkley Books, 2014.

Auerbach, Loyd. *Ghost Hunting: How to Investigate the Paranormal.* Berkeley: Ronin Publishing, 2004.

———. *A Paranormal Casebook.* Dallas: Atriad Press LLC, 2005.

Bagans, Zak. *I am Haunted: Living Life Through the Dead.* Las Vegas: Victory Belt Publishing Inc., 2015.

Bailey, Lynn. *Bisbee: Queen of the Copper Camps.* Tucson: WesternLore Press, 2002.

Beahm, George. *The Stephen King Story: A Literary Profile.* Kansas City, MO: Andrews and McMeel, 1992.

Branning, Debe. *Sleeping With Ghosts! A Ghost Hunter's Guide to Arizona's Haunted Hotels & Inns.* Phoenix: Golden West Publishers, 2007.

"Brewer a Suicide, William J. Lemp Shoots Self Twice Thru the Heart." *The Topeka State Journal,* December 29, 1922, http://chroniclingamerica.loc.gov/lccn/sn82016014/1922-12-29/ed-1/seq-1.pdf.

Brown, Alan. *Haunted Places in the American South.* Jackson: University Press of Mississippi, 2002.

Bryson, Bill. *The Lost Continent.* Harper Perennial, 1989.

Caskey, James. *Haunted Savannah: The Official Guidebook to Savannah Haunted History Tour.* Savannah: Bonaventture Books, 2005.

Christensen, Jo-Anne. *Haunted Hotels.* Edmonton: Ghost House Books, 2002.

"A Civil War Heroine." *The Western News,* December 25, 1901.

Clune, Brian, with Bob Davis. *Ghosts of the Queen Mary.* Charleston: Haunted America, a Division of The History Press, 2014.

Cobb, Al. *Savannah's Ghosts.* Atglen: Schiffer Publishing, 2007.

Connelly, Rita. "The Coolest Small Towns in the U.S.A." *Budget Travel,* March 21, 2006, http://www.budgettravel.com/feature/bisbee-arizona,1564/.

Cooper, Suzanne, et al. *Images of America, RMS Queen Mary.* Charleston: Arcadia Publishing, 2010.

"The Crescent Connection." *Underground Eureka.* Accessed August 2015, http://undergroundeureka.com/crescent-connection.php.

Danielson, Kay Marnon. *Images of America, Eureka Springs, Arkansas.* Chicago: Arcadia Publishing, 2001.

Davis, Susan S. *Stanley Ghost Stories.* Estes Park: Stanley Museum, 2005.

DeBolt, Margaret Wayt. *Savannah Spectres and Other Strange Tales.* Norfolk: The Donning Company, 1984.

Edwards, Walter V. "Jerome Takes Its Medicine II." Jerome Historical Society archives, 1983.

"FAQ: Why Did Sinclar Lewis Decline the Pulitzer Prize?" *The Sinclair Lewis Society.* Accessed September 2015, http://english.illinoisstate.edu/sinclairlewis/sinclair_lewis/faq/faq2.shtml.

Fowler, Gene, and Bill Crawford. *Border Radio: Quacks, Yodelers, Pitchmen, Psychics, and Other Amazing Broadcasters of the American Airwaves.* Austin: University of Texas Press, 1987.

Frederick, Mark C. "Cough, Gasp, Wheeze: The Role of Disease in Jerome's Past." *The Jerome Chronicle,* 2000.

Gagnon, Amy. "Death and Mourning in the Civil War Era." *ConnecticutHistory.org.* Accessed August 2015, http://connecticuthistory.org/death-and-mourning-in-the-civil-war-era/.

Gardner, Renée. *Southern Arizona's Most Haunted.* Atglen: Schiffer Publishing, 2010.

GeorgiaInfo. "James Edward Oglethorpe." Accessed July 2015, http://georgiainfo.galileo.usg.edu/topics/history/article/georgia-as-an-english-colony-1732-1775/james_edward_oglethorpe.

Greenbaum, Leah. "Five St. Louis Ghost Stories That Just Won't Die." *Riverfront Times,* October 25, 2012, www.riverfronttimes.com/stlouis/five-st-louis-ghost-stories-that-just-wont-die/Content?oid=2501495.

Guiley, Rosemary. *The Encyclopedia of Ghosts and Spirits.* New York: Facts on File, 2007.

Hauck, Dennis William. *Haunted Places: The National Directory.* New York: Penguin Books, 2002.

"Heiress, Rewed 2 Weeks Ago, Kills Herself. " *The New York Tribune,* March 21, 1920, http://chroniclingamerica.loc.gov/lccn /sn83030214/1920-03-21/ed-1/seq-7/.

"History, Eureka Springs," accessed July 2015, http://hostelries .eurekaspringshistory.com/crescent_hotel_1886.htm.

"History of the Myrtles Plantation." The Myrtles Plantation, accessed July, 2015, http://myrtlesplantation.com/history.php.

"Joe Namath Sidelines his Historic House." *Atlanta Constitution,* September 16, 1986.

Juhnke, Eric S. *Quacks & Crusaders: The Fabulous Careers of John Brinkley, Norman Baker, and Harry Hoxsey.* Lawrence: University Press of Kansas, 2002.

Kermeen, Frances. *Ghostly Encounters: True Stories of America's Haunted Inns and Hotels.* New York: Warner Books, Inc., 2002.

———. *The Myrtles Plantation: The True Story of America's Most Haunted House.* New York: Warner Books, 2005.

Krygelski, John David. *The Ghosts of the Copper Queen Hotel.* Tucson: Starsys Publishing Company, 2010.

Lee, Adrian. *Mysterious Minnesota.* Woodbury: Llewellyn Publications, 2012.

Lewis, Sinclair. *Main Street.* New York: Bantam Books, 1996.

Lingeman, Richard. *Sinclair Lewis: Rebel from Main Street.* New York: Random House, 2002.

Longbella, Maren. "Is Palmer House Hotel in Sauk Centre Haunted? Spend a Weekend and Find Out." *Pioneer Press*, October 27, 2012, http://www.twincities.com/2012/10/27/is-palmer-house-hotel-in -sauk-centre-haunted-spend-a-weekend-and-find-out/.

Mead, Robin. *Haunted Hotels: A Guide to American and Canadian Inns and Their Ghosts.* Nashville: Rutledge Hill Press, Inc., 1995.

"Medicine in the Verde Valley in 1946." *Verde Village Roundup*, Fall 1983.

Mellen, Greg. "In 33 Years on Queen Mary He's Seen It All." *The Orange County Register,* September 7, 2014. http://www.ocregister .com/articles/queen-633967-mary-ship.html.

"Murder of Anderson Baffles the Police." *Tombstone Epitaph.* February 29, 1920, http://chroniclingamerica.loc.gov/lccn /sn95060905/1920-02-29/ed-1/seq-3/.

Norman, Michael. *The Nearly Departed: Minnesota Ghost Stories & Legends.* St. Paul: Minnesota Historical Society Press, 2009.

Ogden, Tom. *Haunted Hotels, Eerie Inns, Ghoulish Guests, and Creepy Caretakers.* Guilford: Globe Pequot Press, 2010.

O'Neil, Tim. "A Look Back. Lemp Mansion, Home of Beer Dynasty and Suicide." *St. Louis Post-Disptach*, February 12, 2012, http:// www.stltoday.com/news/local/metro/a-look-back-lemp-mansion -home-of-beer-dynasty-and/article_3f697156-1b22-54b8-947c -f582edcf702e.html.

"Our Story." *The Queen Mary*, accessed July 2015, http://www .queenmary.com/history/our-story/.

Pascoe, Jill. *Arizona's Haunted History.* Gilbert: Iron Gate Press, 2008.

Pittman, Rebecca. *The History & Haunting of Lemp Mansion.* Loveland: Wonderland Productions, Inc., 2015.

————. *The History & Haunting of the Stanley Hotel.* Second edition. Loveland: Wonderland Productions, Inc., 2015.

Plath, Sylvia. *Crossing the Water: Transitional Poems.* New York: Harper & Row, 1971.

Price, Ethel Jackson. *Bisbee: Images of America.* Charleston: Arcadia Publishing, 2004.

Pryor, Johnathan. "Interment without Earth: A Study of Sea Burials during the Age of Sail." (Research paper, Duke, 2008), https://twp .duke.edu/uploads/assets/Pryor.pdf.

Rabago, Roberto. *Rich Town Poor Town Ghosts of Copper's Past.* Jerome: Copper Star Publishing Company LLC, 2011.

Rapaport, Diane Sward. *Home Sweet Jerome Death and Rebirth of Arizona's Richest Copper Mining City.* Boulder: Big Earth Publishing Company, 2014.

"REAL Paranormal Investigation and interview at Copper Queen Hotel in Bisbee, Arizona." YouTube video, 9:56, interview with Stephen Hudson, posted by "Paranormal EXP," January 16, 2012, https://www.youtube.com/watch?v=ywV1DeCwB-4.

"Rebirth for an Old Corner." *Savannah Morning News,* August 1, 2003, http://savannahnow.com/stories/080103/LOCfuneralhomes .shtml#.V1sD0UXkBz8.

Ritzert, Anne C. "The Diminutive Giant: William Kehoe." *Savannah News-Press Magazine,* November 16, 1969.

————. "Grand Mansion to be Restored." *Savannah Evening Press,* May 15, 1991.

Robison, Matt Ray. "Main Street, USA." *The Morning News,* May 15, 2014, http://www.themorningnews.org/article/main-street-usa.

Ryan, Tara Kehoe. *Tara Investigates and Films in the William Kehoe House*. August, 8 2009, http://www.taratourssavannah.com/2009 /08/tara-participates-on-new-ghost-intervention-series-at-the -william-kehoe-house/.

Shelton, Richard. *Going Back to Bisbee*. Tucson: The University of Arizona Press, 1992.

Spence, Stephen. "Pure Hoax: The Norman Baker Story." The Crescent Hotel History, July 27, 2013, http://www.crescent-hotel.com /bakerstory.shtml.

Taylor, Troy. *Down in the Darkness. The Shadowy History of America's Haunted Mines, Tunnels & Caverns*. Alton: Whitechapel Press, 2003.

———. *The Ghost Hunter's Guidebook*. Chicago: Whitechapel Press, 2010.

———. *The Haunting of America*. New York: Barnes and Noble Publishing, 2006.

———. *Suicide and Spirits, The True Story of the Rise & Fall of the Lemp Empire*. Decatur: Whitechapel Press, 2014.

Taylor, Troy, and David Wiseheart. "The Legends, Lore & Lies of the Myrtles Plantation," accessed July 2015. http://www.prairieghosts. com/myrtles.html.

Tingley, Al. *Corner on Main Street*. St. Cloud: Dauntless and Creative Concepts, 1984.

Van Praagh, James. *Ghosts Among Us: Uncovering the Truth About the Other Side*. New York: HarperOne, 2008.

Walker, Stephen P. *Lemp: The Haunting History*. St. Louis: Mulligan Printing Company, 1988.

Weinberger, Mark. *Off the Beaten Path: Minnesota.* Guilford: Morris Book Publishing, LLC, 2007.

"Welcome to Bisbee." Bisbee Mining and Historical Museum, accessed July 2015, https://www.bisbeemuseum.org/newsletters /bmbrochure.pdf.

"Where Sick Folks Get Well Without Operation, Radium or X-Ray." Norman Baker, Inc. 1939. Brochure

Whitington, Mitchel. *A Ghost in my Suitcase.* Dallas: Atriad Press, 2005.

"William J. Lemp a Suicide. The Well-Known St. Louis Brewer Kills Himself by Shooting. Grief over the Recent Death of His Son Edward the Supposed Cause of the Act," *The Iron County Register,* February 18, 1904, http://chroniclingamerica.loc.gov/lccn /sn84024283/1904-02-18/ed-1/seq-6/.

Winston, Alvin. *Doctors, Dynamiters, and Gunmen: The Life Story of Norman Baker.* Muscatine, IA: TNT Press, 1936.

Wlodarski, Robert, and Anne Wlodarski. *Queen Mary Ghosts.* Woodland Hills: G-HOST Publishing, 2010.

Woolery, Dr. D.R. *The Grand Old Lady of the Ozarks.* Hominy, OK: Eagles' Nest Press, 1986.

Young, Herbert V. *Ghosts of Cleopatra Hill: Men and Legends of Old Jerome.* Jerome: The Jerome Historical Society, 1964.

———.*They Came to Jerome: The Billion Dollar Copper Camp.* Jerome: The Jerome Historical Society, 1972.

Zeller, Joyce. *Hidden History of Eureka Springs.* Charleston: The History Press, 2011.

Haunted Asylums, Prisons, and Sanatoriums
Inside Abandoned Institutions
for the Crazy, Criminal & Quarantined
JAMIE DAVIS

A chill runs through the air inside the Death Tunnel at Waverly Hills Hospital. The Shadow Man haunts cellblocks at the West Virginia Penitentiary. A Civil War soldier's ghost communicates through flashlights at the Trans-Allegheny Lunatic Asylum. Explore dozens of chilling ghost stories like these and 57 terrifying photographs from ten well-known, haunted institutions across the United States.

Haunted Asylums, Prisons, and Sanatoriums includes the history of each building, personal paranormal experiences from the author and facility staff, and spooky highlights from on-site tours. This spine-tingling, one-of-a-kind guide is filled with photos, historical knowledge, interviews, and frightening first-hand stories. Readers will also enjoy an introduction to basic ghost hunting equipment and detailed information about organizing their own visits to these haunted institutions.

978-0-7387-3750-8, 240 pp., 6 x 9   **$15.99**

OVER 1000 HAUNTED PLACES YOU CAN EXPERIENCE

THE GHOST HUNTER'S FIELD GUIDE

RICH NEWMAN

The Ghost Hunter's Field Guide
Over 1000 Haunted Places You Can Experience
Rich Newman

Ghost hunting isn't just on television. More and more paranormal investigation groups are popping up across the nation. To get in on the action, you need to know where to go.

The Ghost Hunter's Field Guide features over 1,000 haunted places around the country in all fifty states. Visit battlefields, theaters, saloons, hotels, museums, resorts, parks, and other sites teeming with ghostly activity. Each location—haunted by the spirits of murderers, Civil War soldiers, plantation slaves, and others—is absolutely safe and accessible.

This indispensable reference guide features over 100 photos and offers valuable information for each location, including the tales behind the haunting and the kind of paranormal phenomena commonly experienced there: apparitions, shadow shapes, phantom aromas, telekinetic activity, and more.

978-0-7387-2088-3, 432 pp., 6 x 9   **$17.95**

Paranormal Obsession
America's Fascination with Ghosts & Hauntings, Spooks & Spirits
DEONNA KELLI SAYED

Why is America so captivated by the unexplained? Far beyond a book of ghost stories, *Paranormal Obsession* offers a unique cultural studies approach to the global phenomena of spirits, ghost hunting, and all things otherworldly.

Providing an insider's view from within the spiritseeking community, paranormal investigator Deonna Kelli Sayed explores how and why our love of spirits started, how ghosts took over the small screen, the roles of science and religion, our fascination with life after death—and what it all says about American culture.

Weighing perspectives of ghost hunters, religious figures, scientists, academics, parapsychologists, and cast members of the popular TV shows *Ghost Hunters* and *Paranormal State*, this book offers compelling insight into America's fixation on ghostly activity. It also highlights the author's paranormal group's investigation of the USS North Carolina, the most haunted battleship in the United States.

978-0-7387-2635-9, 264 pp., 6 x 9 **$15.95**

Marcus F. Griffin

Foreword by Jeff Belanger

EXTREME
PARANORMAL
INVESTIGATIONS

The Blood Farm Horror,
the Legend of Primrose Road,
and Other Disturbing Hauntings

Extreme Paranormal Investigations
The Blood Farm Horror, the Legend of Primrose Road, and Other Disturbing Hauntings
Marcus F. Griffin

Set foot inside the bone-chilling, dangerous, and sometimes downright terrifying world of extreme paranormal investigations. Join Marcus F. Griffin, Wiccan priest and founder of Witches in Search of the Paranormal (WISP), as he and his team explore the Midwest's most haunted properties. These investigations include the creepiest-of-the-creepy cases WISP has tackled over the years, many of them in locations that had never before been investigated. These true-case files include investigations of Okie Pinokie and the Demon Pillar Pigs, the Ghost Children of Munchkinland Cemetery, and the Legend of Primrose Road. Readers will also get an inside glimpse of previously inaccessible places, such as the former Jeffrey Dahmer property as WISP searches for the notorious serial killer's spirit, and the farm that belonged to Belle Gunness, America's first female serial killer and the perpetrator of the Blood Farm Horror.

978-0-7387-2697-7, 264 pp., 5³/₁₆ x 8   **$15.95**

True Casefiles of a Paranormal Investigator
Stephen Lancaster

As a ghost hunter for nearly fifteen years, Stephen Lancaster's encounters with the paranormal range from the merely incredible to the downright terrifying. This gripping collection of true casefiles takes us behind the scenes of his most fascinating paranormal investigations. See what it's like to come face-to-face with an unearthly glowing woman in a dark cemetery, be attacked by invisible entities, talk to spirits using a flashlight, and dodge objects launched by a poltergeist. Every delicious detail is documented: the history and legends of each haunted location, what Stephen's thinking and feeling throughout each unimaginable encounter, and how he manages to capture ghost faces, spirit voices, a cowboy shadow man, otherworldly orbs, a music-loving spirit playing an antique piano, and other extraordinary paranormal evidence.

978-0-7387-3220-6, 240 pp., 5³⁄₁₆ x 8   **$15.95**

Ghostly Tales
Poltergeists, Haunted Houses, and Messages from Beyond
BILLY ROBERTS

A firsthand witness to an uncountable number of paranormal events, author Billy Roberts tells absolutely true stories that will leave you touched by other worldly fear. Filled with poltergeists, murderers, and hair-raising spirits, *Ghostly Tales* is possibly the most frightening book you will ever read. Some of the spine-chilling stories included in this book are gruesome. Some are horrific. All of the stories will chill you to your very bones.

A dead man lurks in the land of the living, mystifying his family at his own funeral. An unassuming family, caught in the grip of a misbegotten crystal ball, becomes haunted by deplorable scenes of hellish atrocities. A cloven-hooved card shark interrupts a weekly poker game and terrorizes the players with evil foreboding. The dozens of stories in this book are absolutely true, and they all transcend the bounds of the imagination in a way that will have you afraid to turn out the lights.

978-0-7387-3955-7, 216 pp., 5³⁄₁₆ x 8   **$15.99**